Why are Manhole Covers Round?

The renowned Interview Success Guide to help you past the famous Microsoft interview question (or any other job interview you're facing)

Charlie Mulraine

"...an in-depth, humorous and above all practical guide to searching for and getting your dream job."

Carla Cringle, People Manager, Red Bull UK

Why are Manhole Covers Round?

First published in 2010 by Ecademy Press
48 St Vincent Drive, St Albans, Herts, AL1 5SJ
info@ecademy-press.com
www.ecademy-press.com

Printed and Bound by Lightning Source in the UK and USA

Set in Helvetica Neue by Emma Lewis

Printed on acid-free paper from managed forests.
This book is printed on demand, so no copies will be
remaindered or pulped.

ISBN 978-1-905823-80-2

The right of Charlie Mulraine to be identified as the
author of this work has been asserted in accordance with
sections 77 and 78 of the Copyright Designs and Patents
Act 1988.

A CIP catalogue record for this book is available from the
British Library.

All rights reserved. No part of this work may be reproduced
in any material form (including photocopying or storing in any
medium by electronic means and whether or not transiently
or incidentally to some other use of this publication) without
the written permission of the copyright holder except in
accordance with the provisions of the Copyright, Designs
and Patents Act 1988. Applications for the Copyright holder's
written permission to reproduce any part of this publication
should be addressed to the publishers.

Copyright © 2010 Charlie Mulraine

Foreword by
Denys C. Shortt
Chairman, CEO DCS Europe & Enable Software
Winner – Entrepreneur of the Year, Fasttrack 100, Techtrack 100

Dedication:

To my parents Robert and Caroline for their unwavering support and for instilling the belief in me that anything and everything is possible.

Acknowledgements:

Thank you to everyone who provided me with new insights. A special thank you to Fiona Harrold and David Littleford for their invaluable advice and encouragement during the writing of this book.

Contents:

Foreword by Denys Shortt	8
A few words from Charlie…	10
1. Knowing what you want	12
2. The interview magnet – an effective CV	30
3. Writing a powerful covering letter	46
4. Interview preparation	54
5. Preparing for Competency based interviews	74
6. Psychometric testing	80
7. Telephone interviews	84
8. Presentations, assessment centres and role plays	90
9. Face-to-face interviews	102
10. Decision and negotiation time	116
Index	124
The author	126

Foreword

When Charlie approached me to write this foreword, I had to think hard to the start of my own career. My younger days were spent playing international hockey and I always thought I would have a career in sport. However as I matured I started to see new opportunities and I soon became clear on what I wanted to do.

Having this clarity helps to focus your efforts on a defined goal and has been instrumental in the success of my own businesses DCS Europe plc and Enable Software.

This success, especially during these challenging times, is not only down to a robust business plan but also because of the people we have involved in our business. We attract people who combine their skills with a passion for delivering the very best that they can. Our staff care about their work, and especially the service that they deliver, which results in an enhanced experience for our customers.

Clearly not everyone who walks through the doors of DCS for an interview is going to possess this clarity. On some occasions, I am surprised how little people have thought about what they want to do with their careers as well as the lack of detailed interview preparation they have carried out. On reflection, this is not always down to laziness on the part of the candidate but is often down to a degree of naivety.

This book successfully breaks down the job seeking process into well thought out chapters and manageable tips. There really is no excuse for a candidate to be under-prepared since every single aspect of the process is covered, including useful exercises to define your career purpose and a section on typical interview questions.

Although much of the content is written in a light-hearted manner, the messages are serious and practical.

So, why are manhole covers round? Well, future DCS candidates may need to provide me with a suitable answer...

Denys Shortt

Chairman, CEO DCS Europe plc & Enable Software Winner – Entrepreneur of the Year, Fasttrack 100, Techtrack 100

A few words from Charlie…

The purpose of this book is to take the fear out of being interviewed and to give you the tools to be able to approach interviews with confidence and a strong sense of purpose.

It has been an enjoyable challenge to bring together all of the tips and advice that I have gathered over ten years of working in the careers industry. The book has been structured in a way that covers everything from securing an interview to the point of signing your contract of employment. Each chapter is made up of 'bite-sized' pieces some of which may appear flippant at times but I can assure you that each one has an important message. I have deliberately made an effort to write the tips from an employer's point of view and I have not been afraid to unmask some of the strategies that clients adopt when conducting interviews.

We are all guilty of overlooking the fundamentals, especially when we become more proficient in something, and therefore I have aimed to create a guide that you can refer to as your career develops in the future.

If I were only able to give you one 'top tip' then it would be this: remember that an interview is merely a two-way conversation and not an interrogation. It is an opportunity for you to tell your story, to sell your strengths and to communicate enthusiastically your ambitions to someone who wants to listen. In the busy world that we live in today, we are rarely granted this luxury. If you keep this one thought in mind you will be one step closer to the success that you deserve.

And finally, why are manhole covers round? If you ever interview with Microsoft you may need a sensible answer!

Use this book wisely and I wish you every success for the future.

My very best wishes

Charlie

Chapter 1

Knowing what you want

> "There is a giant asleep within every person. When that giant awakes, miracles happen."
>
> **Frederick Faust**

You have polished your shoes, cleaned your teeth, collected your suit from the dry cleaner and have memorised every word in your CV, and yet you are sure that you have overlooked something… perhaps it's the fact that you haven't secured an interview yet! Getting in front of the client is the hardest obstacle to overcome when job hunting, and so this first chapter focuses on everything you need to know for this to happen easily and effortlessly.

Know what you want

For your job search to be successful it is very important to be clear about what you want. This still applies even if you are a more experienced job seeker. It helps to go through a period of self-reflection in order to see how your beliefs, values and ambitions are linked to what you want in life. You don't have to do this alone. Use the expertise of people around you, whether that is trained career counsellors at your school or college, or people that you know and admire in business.

But I don't know what I want!

If you fall into the 'Help!! I have just left University with a degree in something that I have no interest in whatsoever, and I can't justify another year off!' group then a longer period of self-reflection is probably more important then anything else. I will suggest a really good exercise that can give you some clarity. Write a short paragraph that answers the following questions: What excites you? What motivates you? What does your view of life look like? If you could do anything in the knowledge that you couldn't fail, what would that be? This type of self-examination helps to order your thoughts and often uncovers the truth of what you really want.

Still unsure?

If you still can't see the wood for the trees here are some questions that can help peel away a few more layers of uncertainty: What are you able to talk about without ever getting bored? What do your friends and family compliment you on? What does your view of success look like? Are there any people that you admire and if so why?

The bigger picture

What is your opinion of the world we live in? If you had the power to change one thing in the world what would that be? It could be that you hold a deeper passion to affect the world in some way, and bringing this out into the light could create a spark of inspiration about the type of work that would allow you to make this impact. Dream big to live big!

Stuck in a rut

If you wish to change career the above exercise still has value but you may also want to ask yourself different questions about why you feel a change is important. Begin with 'Why am I in the job in the first place?' Knowing 'why you are where you are' helps you to understand the personal circumstances that affect your career choices. Perhaps your personal situation has changed and now your values or priorities are different, requiring you to reassess what a job needs to offer in order to satisfy these changes.

Love and hate

Knowing what you like and what you dislike about your current job is vital in order to start building a picture of your ideal career. There will always be elements of a job that are less appealing than others, and therefore the trick is to get the balance right so that you are motivated by the positive aspects of the role.

Money, money, money!

Whatever our personal values might be, money is an important factor when we choose a career. To make the right choices we need to understand our relationship with money. Not everyone's view of money is the same, and therefore you need to know how much you feel you need to earn and the level of service you are prepared to give in return. If you are already in a job ask yourself the following questions: Do I earn plenty of money in my current job but feel unhappy or under pressure? Do I need to find a way of earning more money? Do I feel trapped in my current job because of my financial responsibilities? Be honest with yourself and don't compare yourself too much with your peers

– it is your life after all, not theirs.

List your talents

Everyone has talents and skills that make them unique. Do you really know what yours are? If you don't, list them now. What positive things do your friends and family say about you? Are you a good listener? Are you good with people? Are you a good organiser? All of these attributes, however insignificant they may seem to you, make you different, and by being aware of them you can choose a career where these skills are seen as an advantage.

Loving your work

From an early age we are led to believe that work and enjoyment are two very different things and are rarely combined. It is therefore not surprising that many people forget their passions in favour of following more traditional career paths. Ask the majority of successful people about their careers and they will tell you that they absolutely love their work. This isn't to say that it's not sometimes extremely tough, but if you love what you do you are more likely to overcome the challenges that you'll face along the way.

Love letters

List all the things that you love doing. What are your passions in life? What gives you fulfilment? Do you prefer the outdoors to an office? Do you love to organise parties? Do you like to help people with their problems? Trust me, you are more likely to feel a greater sense of fulfilment if you are doing something that you love.

Chapter 1

Dream jobs

Most of us dream about what we want in life and in the majority of cases we make up excuses as to why we can't achieve these dreams. Sometimes other people will tell you that your dreams are 'unrealistic'. If this should ever happen, remind yourself that there are countless people who have experienced even greater achievements by changing their careers to follow their true desire. So, I encourage you to write down your dream jobs, however crazy some may seem. Don't think too hard, just let your mind run free and enjoy doing it.

Turning dreams into reality

Write down alongside each dream job how your life would change for the better if it became a reality. How would it make you feel? What advantages would it present to you?

Take action

Then write down the reasons why you haven't pursued these dreams and follow that with actions you could take to overcome them. You never know, one of these dream careers could become a reality.

Become like a guided missile

Okay, now that you are building a clearer picture of what your ideal career looks like, and how it is in line with your view of life and your strengths, the next important step is to make it happen. To do that you need to be specific about what you want and when you want it. The best way to do this is to create short, medium and long term goals that will map out the path you need to follow. Writing down your key career goals not only makes them clear in your mind but also strengthens your commitment to achieving them.

Time is of the essence

Next to each one write down when you want to realise these goals. Adding a time scale for each goal helps to focus your mind on taking the necessary steps to making it a reality. For example, if one of your goals is to secure a job in 2 months you can work back in time so that you know when you need to have secured interviews by, when your CV should be sent, and when you should contact your target companies.

Create a target list

If you are going to be like a guided missile you need to know what your targets are. Your self-reflection exercises will have provided you with some areas of interest. Now is the time to pinpoint companies and individuals you admire in the sectors that especially appeal to you.

Use your personal network

Before we start talking about using recruitment companies to help with your job search, it is important to mention personal networks. Fortunately, networking doesn't have to involve 'pressing the flesh' with strangers wearing name badges and with suit pockets bulging with business cards. Let's look closer to home. Anyone you know is a contact: family, friends, parents of friends, people at your local gym or sports club. Everyone has friends and family and the individuals in these groups have their own networks. Without trying too hard, do you see how big your network could be if you just asked the right questions? Once you have an idea of what type of career interests you, find people within these networks who work in this area or in a related field and talk to them; virtually everyone feels flattered when asked to provide advice or help, so swallow your pride, find your courage and just ask them.

It's not what you know but who you know

The whole point about speaking with people you know is that it is easier and less daunting then calling up strangers or 'cold calling' companies (although sometimes this is unavoidable). Even if an individual doesn't work in your field of interest they may know someone who does and therefore approach all conversations with an open mind. Every person you meet is someone new to add to your network. It is no surprise that the most successful people in this world tend to have the best networks.

Remember your Ps and Qs

When you are asking people for help make doubly sure that you are polite about it. This is important for many reasons. The individuals could be taking time out of their day to help you and are more likely to offer this if they feel it is appreciated. No-one likes to feel pressured and so if your requests are not successful it is best to politely move on to someone else. You may need to come back to this network in the future so ensure that you don't burn any bridges.

Tapping into other people's networks

If you are fortunate enough to access someone else's network remember that your behaviour has a direct impact on them as well. If, when you meet someone from an introduction, you appear disinterested and poorly prepared then I guarantee this news will be passed on to your original contact and they will be less inclined to help you again. However, if you appear enthusiastic and have carried out extensive research prior to your meeting you will be amazed at how many more doors will be opened.

Looking into the future

Remember that one day you will have an enviable network and people will be coming to you for help. What goes around comes around...

Stay alert

Once you have a clear idea of what career you want it is amazing how life can seemingly appear to create moments to move you forward on your way. These opportunities can come at any time, whether you are speaking with friends or strangers, so be alert to them. They are being made known to you for a reason.

Linking in and fun walling

These days many people use online networking groups as well as face-to-face ones to develop contacts. There are business related sites like 'Linkedin' and more socially focused ones such as 'Facebook'. If used wisely they can be extremely useful and can help you to develop contacts quickly and effectively.

Beware Facebook!

This is a fairly new tip and came to my attention when I was speaking to a good friend of mine who works in the field of consulting. His company was recruiting a large number of graduates and he told me that when the HR team were undecided about certain applicants they took a look at their profiles on Facebook to see what they were 'really like'. It sounds like common sense but you will be surprised how much personal and inappropriate information people include on their profile. If you want your page to be like an 'open book' on your life then think about using the privacy settings so that only your closest friends can access the 'expressive' side to your personality. So, be wise about what photos and conversations you include in your profile because, as George Orwell predicted, 'Big Brother is watching you!'

Charlie's Tips to avoid a Facebook Faux Pas

I realise that this may appear rather paranoid but there have been documented stories of people whose careers have been tainted by naïve over enthusiasm on Facebook and other social networking sites. It is really up to you how much of a risk you are prepared to make.

- Make a decision about whether you are going to include clients as friends.

- Choose a profile photo that is unlikely to cause you major embarrassments.

- Choose the personal detail that you include in your profile wisely.

- If you are filling in the "What are you doing at the moment?" during work time, it is probably best not to type in "sitting on my derriere!"

- Keep an eye on what you are doing in 'tagged' photographs.

- Choose your words carefully when writing on other people's walls, especially if you are discussing work colleagues.

- Go to the privacy settings on the home screen. From there, you can determine what information people can access when they search for you, which news feeds and wall postings are visible and who can see your profile and personal information.

Approaching companies direct

There is nothing wrong with using your initiative and approaching companies direct. Many organisations think highly of this approach as it is the best example of your commitment and self-confidence. The tips below cover the many different ways this can be achieved.

Email, write or call?

If you are making a speculative approach to an organisation I would always recommend calling first. You are more likely to build a rapport with someone over the phone rather than by email or letter. It also allows you to ask questions and obtain much more information about the company as well as the names of the key people you need to be contacting. Naturally I suggest that you carry out some research on their company first in order to appear well-informed and credible.

All the fun of the fair

Recruitment and trade fairs offer excellent opportunities to speak with companies directly. On the whole, the exhibiting organisations will have at least one representative from the Human Resources Department attending and I strongly recommend that you ask them about the recruitment process and the key qualities they seek when they employ staff. If you can persuade them to accept your CV, well that's even better.

When is an interview not an interview?

Even though this isn't an interview situation they will be assessing you as if it is. I recommend that you dress the part and wear smart casual or even a suit. I have witnessed fresh grads shuffling around fairs at the NEC in tracksuits and trust me it doesn't look good.

Exhibitor list

Where possible, I strongly recommend contacting the fair organisers for an exhibitor list. If you know who is going to be there you can carry out some background reading beforehand. Any information that can make you appear well-informed is an advantage.

Make yourself heard

Don't worry if the idea of going to one of these events is rather daunting. Remember that all of the companies exhibiting are there to help you, and many of the people on the stands were once in your position. The more people you speak to the more information you will pick up and your confidence will increase.

Be specific

In the same way that you need to be sure about what you want in order to appear purposeful, you also need to be specific about what information you want to obtain at these events. A useful tip is to plan your questions beforehand. Make them simple, open questions; an open question is one that can't be answered with a yes or a no. If you are a graduate you could ask an organisation about their internship programme, the core experience and competencies they seek when recruiting, and the career progression opportunities within the organisation. (We will cover competencies later in the book.)

Keep a record

If you are using many different career hunting methods it is easy to lose track of who you have spoken to. Clearly this can lead to confusion and can possibly harm your chances of success. To avoid this, I recommend that you design a very simple spreadsheet or a table and track your contacts with dates and results of conversations. If you are not computer savvy then delegate this task to a more technically-able friend.

Beware the fading memory

When you are having lots of conversations it can be very easy to forget what each person said. The tracking system above is only of use if you add the information when it is fresh in your mind. If you attend a recruitment fair I recommend that you take a paper and pen with you and during the day write down your comments and action points so that you can enter these into your spreadsheet when you get home.

Chapter 1

Business cards

If this is your first excursion into the job hunting market it is highly unlikely that you possess your own business cards but these don't have to wait for the day you secure a job. Why not get some very simple cards printed with your name, contact details and your key skills and ambitions printed on them. Then when you collect cards at a graduate fair or networking event you can also hand out your own. Now had you ever thought of that before? Don't spend a fortune on gold embossing or high quality paper; save the 'American Psycho' conversations about the quality of your business cards until you are CEO.

Newspapers

Local or national newspapers are an excellent source of information when job hunting. Not only will they have a careers section where opportunities will be advertised but the business sections will provide you with useful market information.

Trade publications

Most market sectors will have at least one magazine that focuses on providing the reader with in-depth information on market trends, companies to look out for as well as the latest opportunities. If you are targeting a specific sector I recommend that you research the best magazines and start subscribing.

Going down the agency route

Working with a respected and well-informed recruitment consultancy can not only be extremely useful but also extremely rewarding. A good agency will be able to provide you with up-to-date market information and if you can build a strong relationship they could help you make future moves in your career. There are thousands of agencies in the market and this can make selecting one that suits your needs seem like a monumental task. To make this appear less daunting, you should begin by asking yourself the most important question: 'Do I need an agent?' If you do, be clear about what you want an agency to achieve for you; it may be that you have enough contacts to manage the job search yourself.

Specialist agencies

Depending on your area of interest, you may need to work with a specialist agency. There are clear advantages to choosing this option, especially if you are looking to work in a niche market. A specialist recruiter should have a deeper understanding of the market and therefore be able to offer you helpful advice to make your search more successful. If it is a company that is well respected in the industry (we will explore this further because this is not always the case) it should also have a solid client base and be able to offer you opportunities that you probably wouldn't be able to source yourself.

The good, the bad and the ugly

It is not always easy to gauge whether an agency is respectable or not, especially if this is your first experience as a job hunter. As someone who has worked in the recruitment sector for over a decade, I am very aware of the poor name that some agencies can give the industry. (One of my clients commented after a successful project, "That was a refreshing change. Previously I had considered all recruitment consultants to be worse than estate agents!" Poor estate agents, they are a much maligned group of people!) Below are a few tips for recognising the agencies with integrity from the ones to avoid.

Call backs

Do they call you back when they say they will? We are not all perfect, but an agency that consistently fails to call you at an agreed time is displaying not only rudeness but a degree of indifference to your situation. You can bet that they are the first on the phone if they think you might be a source of revenue for them.

Providing a job specification

In the majority of cases, a company will have a job specification for the role they are looking to fill. If they don't, then the agency will often work with them to create one that covers the company background, key responsibilities in the role and requirements for a successful candidate. This helps you when preparing for the interview and is also proof that the agency has a close relationship with the client.

Face-to-face or over the phone?

Not all agencies meet their candidates since not all clients demand this. Although this isn't an automatic sign that the agency is not one to work with, an organisation that does take the time to meet you, in order to understand your background, your personality and your ambitions, is likely to be one that is able to represent you in a more professional manner. It also probably works in closer partnership with its clients.

Consultative or dictatorial?

An agency, or consultant with a good standing in the market should be able to offer advice relating to career progression and salary within a sector or a particular organisation. Essentially they are representing their client and you, the candidate, and this means that it is in their best interest to tell you the 'real story' so that you can make an informed decision. It is in no-one's best interest for you to accept a position, only to leave during the probationary period because the role wasn't what you expected. Most Consultants will want to avoid having to negotiate a rebate with a disappointed client, caused by a candidate leaving within this period.

Partnership

A friend of mine who works as a part-time Financial Director describes himself as a 'critical friend' when speaking to his clients. I think this is an excellent phrase and really sums up what a partnership should involve: honesty and support. You should feel that your agent understands what you want and is able to support you and to tell you home truths.

Acting as your project manager

I am not suggesting that you relinquish all responsibility for your job search but a good agency should make you feel that they are managing the recruitment process. By this I mean that you should have been given a clear picture of what you are likely to expect. Let's go through the key stages that they should prepare you for one by one.

Chapter 1

How many interviews?

You should be given a clear picture of how many interviews you will need to attend. A really good agency, where possible, will have pre-booked these dates with the client so that you can plan your diary.

What will the interviews involve?

In addition to the above, the agent should be able to give you detailed information on who you will be interviewed by and their roles within the company. It is in their best interests to ensure that you are properly prepared and therefore you should expect to receive information on what the interview will involve; whether it will be formal or informal, involving any technical or psychometric tests and whether you will need to make a presentation?

Dress and address

We will cover these in slightly more detail later but the agency should, as a matter of course, provide you with an address and information on how to get to the client as well as an outline of what you should wear. There is nothing worse than wearing smart casual when everyone is dressed in suits.

Feedback

A good agency should be able to provide you with feedback after each interview. This should be honest, constructive and include comments on why you were considered suitable or unsuitable, together with suggestions on areas you should work on for subsequent interviews. If they can't, you have to question how strong their relationship is with the client in the first place.

Negotiations

Unless for some reason you would prefer to handle this yourself, it is the agency's job to negotiate the salary and potential start dates on your behalf. It is often easier for a third party to carry this out and the majority of candidates prefer it this way.

Charlie's chapter tips:

- Know what you want.

- List your talents.

- Become like 'a guided missile'.

- Create a company target list.

- Track your conversations.

- Choose your agency wisely.

- Pat yourself on your back – you are on the right track!

Chapter 2

The interview magnet - an effective CV

> "Fix your course to a star and you can navigate any storm."
>
> **Leonardo da Vinci**

You can have a slick interview technique and be the most talented individual in the world but if your CV doesn't reflect this ability these skills will never see the light of day. Getting your CV right is fundamental to successful job hunting. In this chapter we will cover everything you need to enable you to craft a CV that is an accurate reflection of your skills, ability and personality as well as one that acts as an interview magnet.

War and Peace or Jack and Jill?

Nobody wants to read a CV that is six pages long, however well-written it might be! A CV should ideally be no more than two pages long. You need to remember that your potential employer will probably have received 50 to 100 applications for one vacancy and therefore you want to ensure that yours is the one that is read and not put in the 'keep on file' pile. The key points are that it should be easy to read, relevant to the role and provide the client with enough detail about your experience and personality to want to know more.

Structure

It is vital that a CV flows and that the reader feels that he/she is being taken on a journey of your career to date. There are a number of variations on a theme but you will not go far wrong if you use the following CV structure.

Name and contact details

Your name, address, telephone number and email address should appear clearly at the top of the page. Some CVs continue this as a footer on the subsequent pages but this can be overkill. Whether you add 'curriculum vitae' (and please make sure that you spell this correctly) as a title is a personal choice but since it is clear to the reader what they are reading it is not really necessary.

Personal profile

The majority of CVs will begin with a personal profile or personal statement providing the reader with a description of key skills and future ambitions. If I had a pound for the number of profiles that included statements like 'good team player', 'enthusiastic worker' and 'good communicator' I would be an extremely rich man! I appreciate that it is often difficult to avoid certain phrases, but personalise your profile, don't churn out the same words used by so many of the other candidates. Use the words for a reason and make them relevant to you.

Sound bites

If you ever listen to MPs describing a new policy you will notice that they purposefully use powerful, memorable phrases that will be quoted in the media.

Advertisers use the same technique when promoting their products to the public. Create your own sound bite using similar language that makes your experience appealing to the reader.

Test yourself

A good tip to ensure that you only include words with relevance is to imagine the interviewer asking you to justify each one. If you haven't got a reason why you have described yourself in a certain way, don't include it!

"I am a wonderful Manager"

There is nothing wrong with blowing your own trumpet in your personal profile but make sure you can back it up with evidence. Some awkward interviewers, me included, will often pick up on phrases of this kind and will not let them go until the candidate has provided examples and reasons why they think they are so good. In other words, don't fill out your profile with statements that sound impressive unless you can honestly justify them and back them up.

Make it snappy

A personal profile should be a concise description and not an essay. Imagine that you are a product and that an advertising company is trying to come up with a way of selling it to the client. Ask yourself What is the product? What does it do?, How is it unique? and What benefits does it offer to the user? I am not trying to dehumanise you but the ability to 'think outside of yourself' helps you to see what a client sees.

Key attributes

If you have limited or even no work experience at all, don't worry. There are other ways for you to stand out to an employer. If you fall into this category, the employer needs to know: Who you are? What drives you? What successes have you had in life so far? What are your goals? From your earlier self reflection exercises you will have this information to hand. Select five of your key attributes that relate to the key skills highlighted in the job specification, and list these under your personal profile with evidence of how you have demonstrated them in real life. These should be aimed specifically at satisfying the job's requirements. Therefore if the key skills on the job specification included 'customer service' and the 'ability to multi-task', the strengths that you choose should link to these areas. They also need to be measurable. What I mean by that is that listing phrases like 'Project Management' or 'Goal Orientated' are a little meaningless on their own. If instead you wrote 'Proven experience of managing a charity fund raising project at University that successfully raised £50,000 for Cancer Research' forces the reader to pay attention. You can also include any related qualifications.

Education

If you are a recent graduate you probably won't have a tremendous amount of work experience and therefore it makes more sense to include your education and qualifications on your first page, after your profile or achievements section. For the more experienced individual I recommend that this section is added after your work experience since this is what employers are more interested in reading.

A levels and GCSEs

It is common practice now to write '9 GCSEs A-C including English and Maths' rather than listing each subject and grade.

Start at the end or at the beginning?

Always begin your CV with your most recent work experience since this will be the first information that the client will read. Clients may be under intense time pressures when reviewing applications and may skim read your CV.

Bite the bullet

Bullet points are an effective way to list your role responsibilities in a very clear and concise manner. A good tip is to write a short paragraph underneath your job title and dates of employment for each role, that outlines the services provided by your employer and then use bullet points to list each of your key responsibilities and achievements. This helps the reader to put your role into context, especially if they haven't heard of your employer before, and to understand quickly what the key aspects of your role were.

Dots, dashes and numbers

Try to avoid a morse code appeal for rescue! If you are using bullet points then stick to that throughout the CV. Do not use a mixture of bullets, dashes and numbers as it is busy on the eye and looks very messy.

Accentuate the positive

Use of language is something that we will cover in greater detail later but it is important to mention here that you should describe your experiences as positively as you can. People with a positive attitude are arguably more attractive to a client than those with a 'glass half empty' mindset, so ensure that you highlight the good aspects within each role even if you were miserable in the job.

Hobbies and interests

This section allows you to be a bit more informal and show some of your personality and community related activities. It can be as detailed as you like but remember a reader doesn't have a tremendous amount of time so make it interesting and even relevant to the role if you can.

References available on request

It is up to you if you wish to add the names and contact details of your referees at the bottom of the page. It is quite acceptable to simply add 'references available on request'.

Adapt your CV to suit the job

It is perfectly acceptable to shape the content and style of your CV so that it is more relevant to a particular job. I must stress that I am not suggesting that you change dates, academic qualifications or your name! What I mean is that it is common practice for candidates to analyse the requirements of a specific role, and then to stress certain aspects of their experience to suit these requirements.

General pointers

Now that we have the structure in place, below are a few top tips to make sure that your CV doesn't include any howlers.

Dates

On reading a CV, a client should be clear about when a candidate has worked at a particular organisation and for how long. Wherever possible include the month as well as the year. Vague entries, where only the year is stated, can be frustrating for a recruiter or a client and, more importantly, can raise suspicions about the candidate's commercial history. In the same breath, ensure that the dates are in a clear chronological order. Having to explain errors in your CV to a client during an interview can make for a very uncomfortable experience!

Tell the truth and shame the Devil

If a client discovers that you have lied on your CV don't bother booking time off for the next round of interviews. I realise that Sir Alan Sugar was lenient during the recent series of *The Apprentice* but not everyone will be so forgiving.

Blankety Blank

Take a leaf out of Terry Wogan and Les Dawson's book. When you are putting your CV together ensure that you 'fill in the blanks'. Recruiters and employers are suspicious of CVs with long periods of time unaccounted for. If you went travelling, or had a career break don't be afraid to put that down. Include what you gained from these experiences.

A dip in the font

CVs are often updated on a regular basis as people's careers develop; new information is added and content is edited or taken out. Be mindful of keeping the same font and font size throughout your CV as you do this. This is especially important if you are applying for a role where you are required to put together presentations or documents. I promise you the client will pick up on this immediately and you could be 'filed away' in the rejection drawer before you know it.

Eurostile, castellar or porkies?

There are hundreds of different fonts available. The reason why so many have been developed is that each one conveys a particular message to the reader. A CV written in *Jokewood* is perhaps not the most businesslike. Arial and Times New Roman are the recommended ones to use in either 10 or 12 font size. My preference would be to use Arial since Times New Roman can be difficult to read when there is a lot of detail in a CV.

Spell check is not always the answer

Software programmes that correct spelling are extremely useful, but they are not foolproof. Beware of relying completely on spelling software since this can accidentally alter words and completely change the meaning of your sentences.

A labor of love

If you are in the UK and are going to use spell check make sure that you have the setting flagged for UK spelling, otherwise your CV will be 'colorful' and with a distinctly American 'flavor'.

Chapter 2

Always be proffessional...

We are all guilty of making the odd spelling mistake but having spelling errors in your CV is frankly unforgiveable. Misspelling *professional* really is the ultimate howler! Remember that your CV is a reflection of you and your professionalism. Clients and recruitment agencies can be ruthless when spotting errors of this kind. Double check your spelling and double check again. You have permission to ridicule me if I have made errors in this book!

Away in a manger...

Another spelling error that frequently pops up in CVs and application letters is 'Manger' instead of 'Manager'. To say that you are a 'good manger of people' creates some very strange images! I am yet to carry out research to discover whether this happens to a greater extent over the Christmas period.

Grammar

If grammar isn't your strong point ask someone to review your CV to check that your use of language and punctuation is correct. The client is unlikely to be a Professor of English (unless you are really unlucky!) but it is still important to get the basics right. This is essential if the role you are applying for involves a heavy emphasis on written documents and proposals.

Toolazytowork@hotmail.com

If you have a personal email address like the one above fine, but I strongly advise you not to use that as your contact email on your CV. Think carefully about the image that you want to project to a future employer. Your CV is the first piece of evidence about you that a client receives, and therefore they will go through it with a fine tooth comb. Think about it. If you were seeking an energetic employee, bursting with enthusiasm, would you be inspired by a contact email like goodfornothingslacker@hotmail.com?

Answer phones

This is another area that is sometimes overlooked if you are new to the job hunting scene. If you have your landline or mobile number on your CV, ensure that your voicemail message is businesslike. If you are applying for a client- focused role where good customer service is paramount, a message such as "You've heard the beep so you know what to do!" is unlikely to secure you an interview.

Mugshots

Unless the company has requested it, I would recommend not including a photo on your CV. The main reason is that they often end up looking like a passport photograph or worse still like a police mugshot and that won't endear you to anyone.

White space

Putting a CV together is a bit like creating a painting. Okay, this may appear a bit flaky, but all good paintings have a structure and they use the space on the canvas well. In the same way, a good CV uses the white space of the paper to its advantage so that the reader isn't confused by an information overload. Don't be afraid to reduce the amount of information that you include so that the reader can pick out the most relevant detail.

Chapter 2

Regularity is healthy

Another tip is to ensure that the spaces between each section of your CV are regular. The content may be the most important aspect but if your CV is poorly crafted it can create the impression that you are possibly lazy and/or that your attention to detail is sadly lacking.

Repetition, repetition, repetition

Check your profile and work experience part of your CV for repeated words, especially in the same sentence. It may sound a bit pedantic but again it just shows a little extra care to the reader. Repetitions of words make a CV less interesting to read and worse still can suggest that the CV was put together quickly and without much thought. We all require a little help and one of the best reference tools to use is an online Thesaurus.

Long words don't always impress

On the whole, using long words in order to try to impress the reader will backfire. You will either use the word out of context and therefore the sentence won't make any sense, or you will end up sounding like a machine and not a human being. Even though the ability to use a variety of words can prove to the reader that you are possibly creative and imaginative, the majority of employers want staff members who can build rapport rather than a talking thesaurus. Look to use words that relate to the role and the company.

On the 'dog and bone' to 'earn a crust'

It doesn't matter what job you are applying for (unless it is perhaps to secure a role as an *Eastenders* extra) a CV is a formal document and therefore slang should be avoided as much as possible.

Checkmate!

Check and double check your CV and where possible ask a friend or a colleague (perhaps not your current employer!) to read it. Even though you may have double and triple checked it yourself it is extremely easy to miss tiny errors, simply because we often read what we think is there.

Out of body experience

As you are writing your CV always keep to the forefront of your mind who is going to be reading it. Ask yourself whether you would employ yourself from the content and manner in which your CV is presented. Be honest with yourself. If the answer is no, then put in the time and effort to make sure that your CV really does show yourself in the best light.

The elevator pitch

In sales, people talk about the ability to deliver a pitch that is so well-crafted that it can be delivered to someone in the time you travel six floors up in a lift. In the same way, the first page of your CV is your elevator pitch. It needs to convey enough key information for the reader to confidently feel that you have the right experience to warrant an interview. Be self-critical about this aspect of your CV and ask other people's opinion. If it doesn't seem 'punchy' enough, make the suitable changes.

Paper or parchment?

The world has moved on and unless the company specifically requests a paper CV it is generally accepted that the majority of CVs will be sent by email. Consider the format that you adopt to ensure that the reader can easily open the document. I advise using a widely used programme (such as MS Word) or converting it to PDF.

Borders and boxes

One way of separating different sections of a CV is to put the content into different boxes. This can be an effective method but beware of overdoing it. Too many boxes make the page look rather ugly and a thick black border around the outside of your CV can unfortunately make it look like an obituary.

Bold type

A better approach is to use bold type for headings and job titles that will help to differentiate between sections. Again try not to overdo this since bits of bold type scattered here and there can end up confusing the eye which rather defeats the object.

Be creative

Not all jobs require a standardised format for CVs. If you work in a creative field, such as design, this allows you more freedom to create a CV that not only satisfies the need for detail and clarity but also displays your artistic ability. Before going down this route just make sure that the role and company is one where this approach would be suitable.

Imagine your CV belongs to a stranger and ask yourself the following questions:

- Can you describe the personality of the candidate from the information in their personal profile?

- Does the profile provide the answers to what the person does? How they do it? And what makes them unique?

- Do the skills listed give clear examples of how they have been demonstrated by the candidate?

- Are there any gaps in the timeline of the CV that are unaccounted for?

- Are there any unnecessary font variations in the body of the CV?

- Is it clear and easy to read?

- Is the language bold, positive and compelling?

- Does the CV interest you enough to want to meet the individual? If not, why?

- Are there any spelling errors? If so, what impression does that give you as the reader?

- If it is longer than 2 pages, what aspects could be edited?

- If you were only able to describe the individual in one word, what would that word be? If it is not positive, why?

- What does the CV imply about the individual's appearance?

Chapter 2

Charlie's chapter tips:

- Keep it to two pages of A4.

- Don't mix up your fonts or font sizes.

- Most recent work experience should be first.

- Make sure the dates are correct.

- Check your spelling and beware spell check

- Keep your language business-like.

- Ask a friend to double check your CV.

- Now your CV looks better it's on to the letter!

Why are Manhole Covers Round?

Chapter 3

Writing a powerful covering letter

> "I am not on this earth by chance. I am here for a purpose and that purpose is to grow into a mountain, not to shrink to a grain of sand."
>
> **Og Mandino**

Now that you have created an interview magnetising CV, it is time to focus on putting together a powerful covering letter which will make the employer irresistibly drawn to you. Although your covering letter is still a formal document, it does allow you to express more of your personality and to demonstrate your key skills and ambitions.

Put simply, a good covering letter can be divided into three paragraphs. In this chapter we will dissect each paragraph and provide you with the core aspects that need to be included.

Your contact details

At the top of the letter, either centrally placed or top right, you should position your contact details – name, address, telephone number and email address.

Receiver's details

The client's details should be placed underneath your address and to the left of the page. This should include their full name, business title and the business postal address.

All in the title

Although not everyone is precious about their title, it is still essential that you correctly state the title of the person you are sending your CV to. If you are unsure, don't be afraid to call the company reception and ask. I really can't stress enough how this attention to detail can make all the difference.

Dates

The date then needs to be added either above or below the client's address details. This should be in the following format date, month and year, for example 18th May 2008.

Yours faithfully or Yours sincerely?

Don't worry if you are unsure. This is almost a generation question now since we just don't write as many letters as we used to. The simple way to remember which one should be used is to look at who you are addressing. If you have not been given the name of the person then you would address them as Dear Sir or Dear Madam and sign off with 'Yours faithfully'. If you know the name, for example Dear Mr Greene, then you should adopt 'Yours sincerely' to sign off the letter. Simple! It also helps if you had a Great Aunt who was a stickler for correct etiquette!

S.W.A.L.K

Ensure that you maintain the formality when signing off a letter. Phrases such as 'Kind regards', 'All the best', or Best wishes' should only be adopted for emails between friends or once an informal relationship has been formed. Although a client might be touched by S.W.A.L.K., I strongly advise something more business-like.

Paragraph one

This first paragraph puts your application into context by reaffirming what role you are applying for and the reason for your approach. If you are applying for a specific position that has been advertised you will need to state clearly what that position is, where you saw the advert and the reference code if included. If your approach is speculative, the first paragraph needs to inform the reader why you are contacting them. For example:

'A recent article in the Stratford Herald newspaper confirmed your acquisition of two competitor organisations and therefore you may be looking to further strengthen your Sales Division. As a recent graduate with six months sales experience within the retail sector I would be extremely interested in developing my career with your organisation.'

Paragraph two

The second and most important paragraph is where you stake your claim. This needs to make an employer clear about why you are suitable for the opportunity and should contain detailed relevant experience, specific achievements and any qualifications that strengthen your application further. For example:

'I am a newly retired Professional Cricketer who combined his playing career with a full time degree in Business Management from Warwick University. A natural communicator and motivator, my position as Captain required me to make key decisions under intense pressure and to represent the county in a commercial capacity at sponsor networking events. I successfully developed relationships with two leading financial services organisations which led to additional sponsorship revenue for the county and improved services for the players. The county offered me a Business Development role on retiring but I decided to explore more challenging opportunities with organisations offering clearer career progression.'

Paragraph three

The final paragraph should be a short summary of your eligibility followed by a polite close. For example:

'Your business and ambitious plans for the future really excite me, and I believe that my experience, enthusiasm and ability to develop strong relationships would further strengthen your organisation's desire to build a loyal client base amongst the under 25 community.

I enclose my CV and would welcome the opportunity to discuss my future with you in greater detail.'

Autograph

If the company requests a paper version of your CV and covering letter sign your name and then type your name below. If you have doctor's handwriting this is vital.

Typed or handwritten?

Some organisations specifically ask for a handwritten covering letter. If this is the case, ensure that you practise beforehand so that the end product is neatly written and without errors. Receiving a letter with crossings out or layers of thick Tippex is not acceptable!

Chapter 3

Should you dress to the left or right?

Clearly this has no relation to the term used by tailors across the country but concerns the alignment of your text. It is accepted that text should be aligned left or fully justified.

Be positive

As with your CV, the use of language in your covering letter is so important. The words that we use and the manner in which we describe ourselves create an image of who we are in the mind of the reader. What image do you want to portray? Don't be afraid to highlight your successes and achievements! I am not suggesting that you create a false persona but you need to make the reader believe that they have received an application from someone who is capable and confident in their own ability. Use positive phrases and avoid 'wishy washy' words such as 'maybe' or 'might'. Think about how your experience can benefit their organisation. What can you offer them that they may be lacking? Make clear, measurable statements about your experience and then link these to the business you are looking to join. Strong words to use are 'benefit', 'strengthen', 'enhance', 'grow', 'develop', 'exceed'.

Crossing the fine line

There is a fine line between appearing confident and appearing arrogant. The latter can put a reader off an application quite quickly (although this can depend on the industry). Be mindful of the role you are applying for and the culture of the organisation. Stating that you are good or extremely proficient in something is fine but claiming to be 'the best' at something is ill-advised. Would you want to employ someone who claimed to know everything? Advertise your strengths to the reader in combination with your desire to develop these skills further as well as looking to help those around you to develop.

Educate the reader

If you have a disability and you feel the company needs to know about it then state this in your covering letter. This could be important if you require additional tools to help you perform in the role.

Charlie's top tips for covering letters

Imagine you are the employer, and your letter is one of 100s that are piled up on the desk. With that in mind, ask yourself the following questions:

- Is it clearly laid out? If not, how would you change it?

- Is the spelling and grammar correct?

- Is the tone, positive and professional?

- Are there examples of how key strengths have been demonstrated?

- Is the language powerful and authoritative? If not, how could this be improved?

- Does it answer the key requirements in the job spec and/or advert?

- Does it mirror some of the key phrases used by the organisation in the job spec and/or advert?

- What impression does it give of the person behind it?

- Would it stand out from other applications? If not, what changes are needed?

- As well as being professional, does it show a spark of the writer's personality? If not, how could you make it more personal?

Charlie's chapter tips:

- Check the title of the receiver.

- A good letter has three to four distinct paragraphs.

- Use positive language.

- Give examples of specific experience as evidence of your suitability.

- Be clear about why the role and the company are attractive and well suited.

- Use 'Yours sincerely' or 'Yours faithfully' correctly.

- Now you've passed that step it's on to the interview prep!

Why are Manhole Covers Round?

Chapter 4

Interview preparation

"You can have anything you want if you want it desperately enough. You must want it with an exuberance that erupts through the skin and joins with the energy of the world."

Sheila Graham

Being a skilful interviewee is like being a skilful musician or sportsperson; you have to practise at it! An interview room can be a very nerve-wracking place, especially if the questions are incisive and require you to think on your feet. Taking time to practise and prepare for the big day helps to ease the nerves and can make the difference between you receiving that offer instead of the 'We regret to inform you...' letter. Interviews have thankfully moved on from the days of 'gut feelings', although you should still be very conscious of making the best first impression. An experienced interviewer will now ask you for examples of previous behaviour, will question you against selected competencies and possibly even put you through aptitude tests. The following chapters will help to demystify the different interview techniques and provide you with useful tips on how best to prepare for them.

Know thyself!

If there is one person who is expected to know what's contained in your CV then that's you! Take time to read through your CV in detail, making mental notes about how long you worked in each job, memorising the dates and the reasons why you moved on. Bringing a copy of your CV and referring to it whilst you are being interviewed does not go down very well.

Research, research, research!

Companies often open an interview with the standard ice-breaker 'So, tell me what you know about our company?' With information available at the click of a button, it is unacceptable not to know anything about the company you are interviewing with. At the very least take a look at their company website, especially the careers section. This area can provide you with valuable information covering the company's mission statement and key competencies they look for.

Press releases

Another good area to cast your eye over is the recent press releases section. These not only provide you with current market information but can arm you with some interesting talking points to raise in your interview.

Private investigation

Have you ever searched for your own name or someone else's in a search engine? Well, wouldn't it be good to know something about the interviewer? I recommend that you search for their names on the company website first and then try the main search engines. A level of understanding about who is asking the questions not only helps you to create a picture of them before the interview and makes you appear better informed, but also could provide you with information to base questions on. (See, I'm always thinking of you!)

The bare necessities

To make your life even easier here is a checklist of the company information you should have at your finger tips: know when the company was founded, what its core business is, the approximate number of employees, its mission statement, latest news release from their website (if appropriate) and at least two names of competitor companies.

Know the competition

Another favourite interview question is 'Who are our competitors?' Replying with 'I don't know' early on during an interview doesn't do the nerves any good! Make sure that you are one step ahead and find out who the major players are in their sector. If you are feeling really brave call these competitors up and see what services they offer. Letting the interviewer know that you called one of their competitors to see how their services differed puts you in the 'A' list group of candidates. Having this information at your finger tips can be extremely powerful and will count in your favour.

Search engines

Using a well known search engine (such as Google, Bing or Yahoo) is another efficient way to find out about a company's history. Take your time, and look at the associated links as you may pick up some useful information that you can use during your interview.

Remember, extra research will help you stand out from the crowd and increase your credibility.

Use your network

Go back to your professional network and see if you know anyone who works in the same sector as the company you are interviewing with. Call them up and ask them if they know about the company. They may even know someone who works there. I can assure you that you will be astounded how networks are linked.

Trade press

The majority of industries will have an associated trade magazine or online journal. If you really want to do your homework, reading through these will provide you with market news and possibly even specific detail on your potential employer.

Keeping with tradition

The traditional style of interview is one in which an interviewer will go through your CV, often in reverse order, and ask specific questions relating to your experience in each particular role. As we covered in the last chapter, it is essential that you are not only confident about when and where you worked, but also why. The interviewer will be interested to know the reasons behind certain career choices and what your ambitions were at that time. To discuss this competently, you will need to take yourself back to the time that you made those decisions and make a mental note of what you were experiencing then. The more information you can provide your interviewer, the more they will be convinced that you have taken control of your career and shaped it to suit your personal goals.

Should I bring a CV to the interview?

I am sure that there are different viewpoints on this question and I have touched on that in chapter 2. My advice would be to take a copy with you if you have to, but keep it in a folder and leave it there during the interview unless the client asks you for it. The client should be well-prepared and will already have a copy with them. I have interviewed candidates that have constantly referred to their CVs during an interview and it can make building a level of rapport quite difficult. It acts as a distraction and hinders the candidate rather than helps them. It also makes the interviewer doubt the candidate's knowledge of his/her own career.

Dodging the awkward question

You can be sure that if there are any questions that you really hope your interviewer won't ask, they will be on his/her list! My advice is to write all of these potential questions down, to prepare as if you were to face Jeremy Paxman on *Newsnight*, and have some very good answers at the ready.

Pencils have erasers because no-one is perfect

All of us have areas that we would like to improve and you can be confident that the majority of interviewers will want to know what they are. Being asked "What are your 3 main weaknesses?" is a standard question with many organisations. The first piece of advice is to know them yourself and list them during your interview preparation. The art is to give an honest answer that demonstrates that you recognise the problem and that you have methods that lessen its effect. For example, if your weakness is that you find it difficult to delegate tasks your answer could be "Having been extremely hands on in my previous role, initially I found it a challenge to delegate tasks to my new team. To improve this I made a conscious decision to take more time to understand the strengths of each individual and to give them responsibility for tasks that would challenge and motivate them."

The case for the defence

A really powerful exercise to combat nerves and boost your confidence before an interview involves imagining that you are in a court of law (not the most relaxing of scenarios, but bear with me.). The case is whether you are suitable for the position you are interviewing for and it is now your turn as the Defence Lawyer to step up and deliver your closing argument as to why you are the right person for the job. Think about the direct language lawyers use and how they always back up their statements with evidence. Put pen to paper and begin with "I am a highly skilled individual and good enough to secure the role of [add the position here] for these core reasons… (include at least five reasons, each supported with evidence)."

Final preparation

People make up their minds about the quality of a website in the blink of an eye. In the same way, research has shown that someone will form judgements about you after only four minutes of clapping eyes on you, so make sure that your interview starts off on the right foot by taking the time over your appearance.

Chapter 4

You are comfortable with all the detail contained in your CV, have studied the company website and rehearsed your answers to potential questions. It is now time to carry out the final preparations that will make you stand out from the crowd. Some of the following steps will be obvious to you but often it is the simple things with the most impact that we overlook, and therefore read and really understand the messages in the following steps.

Richard Branson or Robin Day?

There is a growing trend for men these days to wear a suit without a tie. Although this is acceptable in many organisations, the safest option, especially if you are uncertain about the company dress code, is to wear a tie. The wearing of a bow-tie is a particularly flamboyant statement and you do so at your peril!

Get knotted

If you make the effort to wear a tie you should also ensure that you tie it correctly. An undone top button with a tie around the navel will not impress.

5 o'clock shadow

It may be ok for George Michael but make sure that you have shaved before meeting the client.

The sweet smell of success...

Now, this is a slightly sensitive topic – personal hygiene! Interviews are often held in confined spaces, where the interviewer and interviewee are in close proximity to each other. Make sure that your 'personal grooming' is never the reason for an interview being cut short. There are many causes of bad breath and one of these is dehydration. This combined with cigarettes and coffee can create a pungent cocktail. Checklist: shower, use deodorant, don't overdo it with the aftershave/perfume, clean your teeth, drink plenty of water and leave the coffee and cigarettes (or give up!) until after the interview.

Excuse me, but can you tell me how to get to London please?

As daft as it may sound, every single day there will be a candidate who manages to get lost on the way to the interview. Make sure you don't add yourself to that list. Check the address with the company reception and plan your route in advance. If you have to drive or take a train find out what the traffic is like at the time your interview will be held and check timetables for possible cancellations. There are few feelings that are worse than the panic of arriving late for an interview. If you have a disability it is also a good idea to check with the company reception whether the building has appropriate access points.

Anecdote

Some of these tips are born out of personal experience. A few years ago, I arrived nice and early for a client meeting in London. I had researched the company and was feeling relaxed and confident. It was only after I had been sitting in the reception for 10 minutes that I got a strong feeling of 'something not being quite right'. When the receptionist said that she was struggling to locate the client in the building it was then that I realised what it was: I had arrived a whole day early! The only thing that made me feel any better was that the client (who very kindly agreed to see me anyway) informed me without any embarrassment on his part that he had once arrived for a meeting a whole week early!

What's in a name?

Make sure that you write down the name of the person you are meeting with. An extension of this tip is to look up their name on the company website as there might be an online personal profile. This is a great way to build an even greater rapport as well as demonstrate to the interviewer that you have done your homework.

Suit or smart casual?

My advice is to always wear a suit for men and either a suit or blouse with smart trousers/skirt for women unless the interviewer has stated otherwise. It is easy to make an assumption that a company is informal and casual (especially if it is in the new media sector) but this isn't always the case. The wearing of a suit creates an image of professionalism and care. It is far better to adapt your dress once you're in the job than be turned down for appearing too slovenly.

The 'sniff' test

Rummaging around in the bottom of the laundry basket for your lucky interview shirt/blouse is not a great way to begin the day so please don't do this before an interview. Plan what you are going to wear in advance and make sure that everything is clean and fresh.

Razor sharp creases

The policy on wearing ties may have relaxed with some companies but that doesn't mean you can turn up in a shirt/blouse that looks as if you have just slept in it!

Ensure that you give it a proper iron the night before – that includes the front and not just the collar and cuffs.

Spit and polish

I assure you that I am not suggesting that you turn up to an interview looking like one of the Queen's Lifeguards but polished shoes are important. A smart suit and freshly ironed shirt/blouse can be ruined by a pair of scuffed or muddy shoes. If you can, buy a pair of shoes purely for work situations so that they avoid the usual wear and tear, and ensure that they are well buffed. The army use cotton wool, polish and saliva but I suggest that a stiff brush with some Kiwi polish will suffice.

Saturday night fever

We all have our own fashion sense but sadly not everyone will appreciate our tastes. During your preparation you should have gained a clear picture of the company's working practices and the type of image they look to promote to their customers. A good tip is to try to mirror this image. To some of you this may sound like capitulation and a betrayal of your individuality but this subtle approach immediately improves your chances of building rapport with the interviewer. Once you are in the job you can be more confident about what is acceptable or not.

Waxing lyrical

You may have a weekend hairstyle where someone could be mistaken for thinking that you have shoved your fingers in an electric socket, but think hard about whether this will go down well at work. I know that I sound like your parent, but some work environments can be a little bit judgemental. This entirely depends on the sector. Many creative environments will want to encourage expression and individuality whereas financial services in general look for a more traditional business-like appearance. This is most applicable to roles that are client-facing. Think about what the company is representing and the types of people they are providing services to. What are the clients expecting? What sort of image would strengthen their feelings of reliability and trust? Ultimately it is your personality, enthusiasm and professionalism that are the most important factors in any job that you perform, and these should never be underestimated, but a few subtle adjustments can make a positive difference during the interview.

Clean cuticles

This is aimed more at men than women. Unless you are an acoustic guitar player make sure that you have cut your nails and ensure that they are clean.

Visualisation

Many elite performers including NASA astronauts and leading sportspeople have used visualisation and mental rehearsal techniques for a number of years to enhance their performance. We have already talked about practise and how that improves performance; well you can actually practise without physically carrying out the action. There is compelling evidence that suggests that using your imagination to mentally rehearse a future task not only increases confidence but can also help to produce a more successful result. So, I strongly recommend that the night before your interview you find a quiet space, turn off your phone, close your eyes and visualise each part of the interview. Use your imagination and see yourself in your mind's eye greeting the interviewer confidently by the hand, and the calm manner in which you answer his/her questions. It is important to stress that you should mentally rehearse as if the interview is happening in the present and not as if it is a future event and that you should <u>only</u> imagine a positive outcome. If this technique enabled astronauts to land on the moon it will definitely have a positive impact on your interview success.

Question the questioner

At the end of virtually every interview the interviewer will ask you if you have any questions that you would like to ask. The purpose of this is not only to ensure that you walk away with all the information you need but also to see whether you have carried out research into the company and considered the role more deeply. I strongly recommend that you prepare these beforehand since crafting insightful questions in the heat of an interview can be extremely difficult. To help you, I have listed, on the following pages, 20 thought-provoking questions to ask.

Charlie's top 20 questions to ask at interview:

1. What is the potential career progression with this position?
   Charlie's tip – This demonstrates that you are ambitious, as well as displaying an interest in a potential long term future with the organisation.

2. How will the role develop over the next 6 to 12 months?
   Charlie's tip - As above, this question is proving to

the interviewer that you are a long term thinker.

3. Is there an opportunity for me to shape and develop the role?
Charlie's tip – This question suggests that you are someone who likes to take the initiative. It is a good question to ask because it may further or even lessen your interest in the position. If you like the freedom to be able to make decisions but the opportunity to do so is limited it may be that the role is not the right one for you.

4. Personal development is very important to me. What training programmes does your company invest in?
Charlie's tip – This question will highlight whether the hiring company invests in its people. Specific qualifications may be of particular interest to you, and therefore this will be an important question for you to ask.

5. What is the selection process following this interview and the related timescales involved?
Charlie's tip – This information enables you to manage expectations. It may be that you already have an offer, and therefore if their selection process is too lengthy you are in a position to make the right decisions.

6. What are the key competencies required for this role? (Only ask if they haven't been covered during the main interview.)
Charlie's tip – If these haven't been covered in detail, it is important to be sure about what key strengths they see as being the most important. Knowing these allows you to state your suitabil-

ity more confidently.

7. How would you describe the perfect candidate? (Only ask if it hasn't been made clear during the interview.)
Charlie's tip – Job specs can be rather generic. If the interviewer is the Line Manager, it is good to have the ideal candidate described in their own words.

8. Can you describe the personalities of the people in the team and how they work together?
Charlie's tip – Having an insight into the dynamics of the team enables you to start planning how you would build rapport with them. This is especially important if you are going to be managing them.

9. Is it appropriate to ask your view of my suitability now? (Some interviewers don't want to be put on the spot and prefer to consider their opinion.)
Charlie's tip – This question requires a bit of 'feel'. If you think you have built up a good rapport with the interviewer they should feel happy giving you an answer. If the interviewer is a little more guarded, treat this question with caution.

10. What is the review process for employees and how often do they take place?
Charlie's tip – A company that holds regular reviews with its staff clearly values them highly.

11. What do you think the most challenging aspect of this role will be?
Charlie's tip – This information may give you a better understanding as to what to expect and whether you feel the role is right for you or not.

12. Are there any new services or business areas you are looking into?
    Charlie's tip – This proves to the interviewer that you are able to see the bigger picture. It may be that you have expertise or an interest in areas they are looking to expand into.

13. What is the company strategy moving forward?
    Charlie's tip – As well as showing your interest in the business as a whole, the answer will also help you to see whether a long term future with the company would be attractive.

14. Is this a new position or is the current person moving on?
    Charlie's tip – The answer to this question is very important. If you are replacing someone, it is good to know why they are leaving and whether this individual experienced any challenges or issues in the position.

15. Is there any danger that this role could be put on hold?
    Charlie's tip – If this is a possibility, it is better that you know sooner rather than later.

16. How long have you been with the organisation and what do you enjoy about working here?
    Charlie's tip – It is useful to understand the motivations of the person interviewing you, especially if they have been with the company for a long time. By listening to the language they use, you can gain a clear picture of the company's culture.

17. What in your view makes this company different

from others in the same sector?
Charlie's tip – As above, it is interesting to get this view from someone within the firm. Be prepared for them to ask the same question back!

18. How would you describe the working environment?
Charlie's tip – This is another question that enables you to paint a more detailed picture of the company.

19. Does the company organise any staff social events?
Charlie's tip – The question should give you evidence about the work/life balance within the company. Be careful not to make it appear as if you are only interested in after work drinks!

20. Is there the potential for any travel in the role?
Charlie's tip – It may be that travel is attractive to you, or possibly it could make the position less appealing.

Charlie's top 20 interview questions to be mindful of!

1. What are your weaknesses?
Charlie's tip – The interviewer is looking for honesty as well as an understanding of how you combat your weaknesses. With this in mind your answer should end with a positive statement.

2. What do you feel we could improve as an organisation?
Charlie's tip – Do your research and ensure that all comments are constructive and as positive as

possible.

3. Why did you leave your last job?
   Charlie's tip – Be honest and non-evasive and ensure that you don't speak negatively about your previous employer.

4. What is your view of your current employer and the way it does business?
   Charlie's tip – Again, do not concentrate on the negative aspects and instead highlight the positive impact there has been on your career.

5. Tell me about your biggest failure?
   Charlie's tip – This tests your ability to be open about areas of weakness whilst also seeing how you have learnt from the experience.

6. What do you know about our company?
   Charlie's tip – The best way to answer this question is to weave facts from the website with information you have found from your research. They will expect more from you than a regurgitation of the information from their Home page and so select specific details that demonstrate the depth of your research.

7. How do you deal with criticism?
   Charlie's tip – The interviewer wants to know whether you can deal with criticism without taking it too personally and whether you can learn from these experiences positively.

8. What motivates you?
   Charlie's tip – Enthusiasm and passion are drivers for success and therefore the interviewer wants to

know what gets you out of bed in the morning.

9. How would your current employer describe you?
   Charlie's tip – This is another question that tests your self-awareness and your ability to see yourself through other people's eyes. As with the majority of questions you should give precise positive answers.

10. Why should we employ you?
    Charlie's tip – This is a perfect opportunity to sell yourself. Use strong, persuasive language with evidence to support your points.

11. How do you see your career developing in 5 years' time?
    Charlie's tip – Most employers like candidates who have thought about their careers. You don't need to be specific but you need to demonstrate that you have considered your future.

12. What kinds of people do you have difficulty working with?
    Charlie's tip – The interviewer wants to know whether you are able to work with different kinds of people but at the same time will want to know how you combat any difficulties you have had with certain personality types.

13. Why do you want this job?
    Charlie's tip – The interviewer is looking for a compelling argument that links your motivations to your values and ambitions and that shows how these can be satisfied in the position offered.

14. Do you have any concerns or reservations about

the role?
Charlie's tip – Think very hard about this one. If you are unsure be mindful not to commit an answer that you may regret later. If you do have concerns then make your comments constructive. Worrying about the length of the lunch break will not go down very well.

15. What interests you least about this job?
    Charlie's tip – As above, make your comments constructive without dwelling on the negative. If there isn't anything that doesn't interest you, let them know.

16. What makes you frustrated at work?
    Charlie's tip – Everyone gets frustrated at work and it may be that the company can reduce potential frustrations if you are honest with your answer. Beware though and ensure that you demonstrate how you deal with these frustrations positively.

17. How do you deal with conflict?
    Charlie's tip – Conflict is unavoidable in a team environment. The interviewer wants to know if you are able to resolve disputes whilst still being able to state your position firmly. Do you isolate people or can you respect different opinions?

18. What's your impression of the company so far?
    Charlie's tip – If you have been given a tour of the offices you should comment on the atmosphere and on the impressions left on you by the people you have met. Once again, be positive!

19. Who do you admire and why?
    Charlie's tip – Here the interviewer is interested

to know what qualities you see as being most important to you. It may be that these are qualities that they value highly as well.

20. Do you prefer working by yourself or with others? Charlie's tip – If the role involves working within a team than clearly an answer implying that you don't enjoy teamwork will not be well received. Ultimately you need to answer honestly but an ideal reply would be that you enjoy the support and motivation of working within a team whilst you are also focused enough to be able to work on projects alone.

Charlie's chapter tips:

- Be confident about the detail in your CV.

- Research the company and its competition.

- Dress appropriately.

- Write down the names of the interviewers.

- Plan your journey.

- Prepare for the awkward question

- Close your eyes and visualise.

- Prepare well-considered, intelligent questions.

- That was a breeze, now hold tight for competencies!

Chapter 5

Competency based interviews

> "It's never too late to be what you might have been."
>
> **George Eliot**

A competency is a behaviour that a candidate must have, or be able to acquire, in order to succeed in a role, whereas competence refers to a system of minimum standards that need to be achieved. Nowadays, the majority of organisations will break each vacancy down into a number of core competencies, and candidates will be asked questions requiring them to show evidence of demonstrating them.

Be competent about the competencies

The secret is to know what the competencies are before your interview. If they are not listed in the job specification, which should be the case, the next best place to search is within the Careers section of the company's website. If you are still struggling to find them, you are perfectly entitled to ask the company or the recruitment consultant (if you have gone via an agency) before your interview.

Key competencies

According to a recent survey by the Chartered Institute of Personnel and Development, the most popular competencies interviewed against by clients are:

- Communication skills.

- People management.

- Team skills.

- Customer service skills.

- Results-orientation.

- Problem-solving.

What does a competency question sound like?

Okay, so we now know what a competency is but what does a competency question actually sound like? Well, there are two tell-tale signs to look out for. If you can't answer yes or no to it and it is asking for a real-life example of something you have done in the past, it is more than likely to be a competency based question. Let's refer back to the list of top six competencies and we'll go through them one by one and provide an example question for each one.

Communication skills:

Q. Give me an example of a time when you have had to explain a new idea of yours to a group of people? How was your idea received?

Q. Give me an example of a time recently when you have needed to influence someone? What were you trying to achieve?

People Management:

Q. Give me an example of when you have had to organise a team and rely on them to perform a complex task?
Q. Talk me through a specific example of when you have helped a member of your team improve their skills or performance?

Team skills:

Q. Tell me about a time when you have had to join a new team/group? What did you do to make sure that you were accepted by this group?
Q. Give me an example of when you have disagreed with a team majority decision? What did you do? And how did you react?

Customer Service Skills:

Q. Give me an example of a situation where you have had to deal with customer dissatisfaction?
Q. Tell me the most significant improvements that you have introduced into your organisation that have made a direct impact on the customer?

Results Orientation:

Q. Give me an example of where you have been set a specific goal? What was it and how did you achieve it?
Q. Talk me through the targets you have been set this year and the methods you adopt to achieve them?

Problem solving:

Q. Give me an example of a difficult problem you have dealt with. What were you trying to achieve?
Q. Give me an example of a problem you were unable

to solve? What was it and how did you react?

STAR - Situation or Task, Action, Result

We now know what a competency is and what a question sounds like. But how do we answer one? If you look at the questions above, there are clues in the way that they are phrased. If you are new to competency or behavioural style interviews, a useful mnemonic to remember is STAR. This stands for Situation or Task, Action and Result. When you are asked how you demonstrated a specific competence in the past allow yourself a pause and think, What was the situation? What task did I perform? What action did I take? and What was the result of that action? If you follow this simple process you will provide the interviewer with all the evidence they need.

What is the point of them?

The idea behind this style of interviewing is that it forces you to give real examples of how you have acted and behaved. In some types of interview you may be asked What would you do in this situation? This doesn't require any evidence, and makes it possible for you to give the answer that the interviewer wants to hear. With competency-based interviews the past experience can provide the interviewer with evidence of possible future behaviour.

Running out of examples?

Every interviewer will appreciate that you are not a robot. At some time during the interview there is the chance that you will not be able to think of a suitable example. The best tip in this instance is to remember TCUP (Thinking Clearly Under Pressure), a mnemonic that Sir Clive Woodward instilled in the 2003 World Cup winning England rugby team. Take a deep breath, take your time and calmly think through your relevant experience for an example. If you still can't think of an example let the interviewer know and either give an example of a situation that is similar or ask if you could revisit that question later in the interview.

Off the cuff

Competency-based interviews are the toughest ones in which to perform well if you haven't done your preparation adequately. The ability to think on your feet and provide detailed and relevant answers if you haven't prepared well is almost impossible. Make sure that you take the time to think of really good examples of where you have satisfied these competencies in your work and everyday life. A sound bit of advice is to try to come up with at least three examples for each competency that can be used on the day.

Practice makes perfect

It was the great South African golfer Gary Player who said "The harder I practice the luckier I get!" This mindset applies to most aspects of life, and interviews are no exception. I strongly recommend that you go through a 'dummy interview' with a friend. Explain to them the nature of the interview and you can even provide them with appropriate questions to ask you. If the interview was organised by an agency you can ask the consultant to go through this with you instead. It doesn't matter that it is not a formal interview situation. The important aspect is hearing yourself answering the questions. Be self-critical and ask yourself whether you sounded confident and convincing. It is easier to make changes on the practice ground than on the day.

Charlie's chapter tips:

- Know what the company's competencies are.

- Create questions for each competency.

- Come up with at least three examples for each question that satisfies that competency.

- Practice delivering your answers to a friend.

- An interviewer's approach can be eclectic, so let's prepare for psychometric!

Chapter 6

Psychometric testing

"The question is not 'who am I?' but 'who do I want to be?'"

Fiona Harrold

Cogito ergo sum

Psychometric testing doesn't mean that by giving the wrong answers you will be sent to the 'funny farm'! The aim of this method of assessment is to discover how you think and react under various circumstances e.g. in group situations and when under pressure. The secret to carrying out these tests is to remain calm and answer instinctively. Remember that there are no right or wrong answers. The answers are personal to you, and therefore it is recommended to go with your gut feeling rather than trying to give the answers you think the company wants to hear. In the majority of cases employers will use the information gathered from these tests in a positive way to make sure that they know how best to motivate you, manage you and understand you.

Always read the small print

Even though instinctive responses are more likely to be in line with your core values, you should always take time to read the instructions carefully so that you fully understand what is being asked of you.

Don't second guess

The creators of psychometric tests are, unsurprisingly, cunning foxes! They will often ask the same question in a variety of different ways so don't try to give the answer you feel they are looking for because it will be obvious to them and your results will irregular; if this happens they may well ask you to retake the test. The results of these tests are there to give an indication of your personality type and therefore will raise points for discussion during the interview itself. It will be rare for you to be discounted purely based on your psychometric results.

It takes all sorts

It is worth remembering that a client might be looking for a number of different personality types for their team and therefore your attributes might be exactly what they need to build a successful unit.

The results benefit you

Psychometrics are primarily used to see whether your personality type suits a particular role or organisation and therefore it really is to your benefit that you answer honestly. It may be that the position isn't right for you and it is better to have this highlighted at an early stage. In another instance the tests may pinpoint areas of development that the organisation could help you with.

Types of Psychometric tests

There are many providers of psychometric testing tools and below are the main players.

Thomas International has been providing assessment

testing tools for over 25 years. Their system tests three main areas: personality and behaviour; aptitude, ability and skills; and job profiling and human job analysis. Their Personal Profile Analysis (PPA) test involves 24 questions. For each question there are four adjectives and you will be required to indicate which one most and least describes you.

The Myers Briggs Type Indicator identifies four basic preferences in people's behaviour, providing a framework that allows a better understanding of the behaviour of yourself and others. It is often used in team building as well as the recruitment process.

The Occupational Personality Questionnaire (OPQ) devised by SHL is one of, if not the most widely used psychometric measure in the world today, providing objective information on your predicted behaviour in the workplace, how you work with other people as well as highlighting the most suitable careers options.

The Wave is a relatively new product in the psychometric marketplace and was developed by Peter Saville, previously the founder of SHL Group. The questionnaires have been designed in order to assist organisations with their understanding of your motivations and attributes and how these will interact within their workplace culture.

Challenge

If you disagree with the findings of the test, don't be afraid to challenge them during the interview. It may be that you misread one of the questions, or that you thought too hard about your answer. Remember, that the conclusions of the test are there to be discussed and are not final. Don't be worried if you are asked to complete another test. Sometimes companies will ask you to do this if the result does not appear to reflect your personality.

Charlie's chapter tips:

- Read the instructions carefully.

- Answer instinctively – go with your gut feeling.

- Keep calm. You will not be sectioned!

- Be true to yourself.

- Avoid the temptation to 'second guess' the question.

- Now let's move out of the Twilight Zone and onto the telephone!

Chapter 7

Telephone interviews

> "Nurture your mind with great thoughts; to believe in the heroic makes heroes."
>
> **Benjamin Disraeli**

In many cases an organisation might arrange a telephone interview with you before committing to a face-to-face meeting. The very fact that this approach seems slightly less formal can put you off guard. The most important thing to remember is to prepare as you would for a face-to-face interview. The following tips will prevent you from falling into this trap and will ensure that the client has the pleasure of meeting you in person.

Beware the Bermuda Triangle

I am sure that we have all experienced a loss of reception during a mobile phone call. This can be disconcerting when in the middle of an interview and so where possible give the company a landline number to call. You will come across as being far more professional and it will also ease your nerves since you know you won't be cut off.

Switch off your mobile

If you are going to talk to the client on a landline the last thing you then want is for your mobile to ring during the call, especially if you have Jay-Z *99*

Problems as your ringtone! Turn it off or change the tone to silent.

Do not disturb

Make sure that you choose a time when you know you won't be disturbed. Choose a room in the house where you feel comfortable and where you can think clearly. If you are relaxed in your surroundings then you will sound relaxed and confident over the phone.

Turn off all TVs, radios and stereos

To avoid the client having to compete with a dramatic episode of *Dr Who* or *Eastenders* switch off all TVs and stereos.

Being hounded

If you have any pets it is worthwhile putting them in a part of the house where they will not disturb the call or if this isn't possible ask a friend to look after them for the duration of the call.

Children should be seen and not heard

Do your level best (within the law!) to keep any children quiet and it's probably best not to allow them to answer the phone for you – unless you feel they are likely to give a better interview then you!

Prepare your content

One of the advantages of being at the other end of a telephone is that you can refer to facts, figures and key answers without being seen. At least thirty minutes before the call gather all your key information together and layout in front of you the key points that you want to talk about. Make sure that the information is clear and easy to refer to. You don't want to sound as if you are reading answers over the phone, especially if you stumble over your spidery handwriting.

Rehydrate

I once gave a 10 minute educational presentation on the effects of dehydration which was received with derision! It may sound odd but being well-hydrated is really important. Any athlete will tell you that being dehydrated affects your ability to think and react quickly. A glass of water before your telephone interview will also lubricate the vocal cords and prevent you from sounding like Phyllis from *Corrie*.

Be on time

It is vital that you are ready and waiting by the phone at the allotted time. It is extremely unprofessional not to be there and some companies won't give you a second chance. If for any reason you are not going to be able to answer the phone then let the client know as soon as you can. If you are going through an agency then it is courteous to let the consultant know as well.

St. Mary Mead 363555

The days of answering the phone like Miss Marple (showing my age) have long since passed, however it is still very important to answer professionally. It may be that the client calls you earlier than expected which could throw you off guard. Therefore ensure that you answer clearly and confidently. Picking up the phone with a 'Yo dude!' is unlikely to impress. Answer the call with a confident 'Hello' with your name.

Answer phones

We have covered this earlier in the book but it is relevant to highlight the importance of having a professional and welcoming mobile voicemail message just in case you are on the phone at the time of the call. I have heard of some candidate applications having been immediately discounted due to their unprofessional voicemail message. So be warned.

Ciao for now

The language you use during a telephone interview is probably even more important than during a face-to-face interview. Since you can't be seen, the interviewer will be focusing on how you express yourself and whether it is appropriate for the role you are being interviewed for. Remember that you are not speaking with a friend and therefore demonstrate a degree of respect and formality.

Mind the gap!

As well as being made aware of this on the underground it is also extremely relevant for telephone interviews. As above, it is important to remember that not being in front of the client can create communication challenges and one of these is filling in gaps in conversation. It is tempting enough during a face-to-face interview to believe that all gaps need to be filled by you and I can assure you that this feeling is exaggerated when speaking over the phone. My advice is to be clear with your answers and to only fill gaps if you have something worthwhile to say. Some interviewers will be crafty and will deliberately insert gaps in the conversation in order to see how you react. Be mindful about this but don't take it to the extreme and create a battle of the pregnant pauses.

It doesn't cost a thing to smile

Smiling can be overlooked by many during telephone interviews, purely because candidates feel that if it can't be seen it is unimportant. The magical thing about a smile is that it makes someone sound much warmer and more approachable even over the phone.

Be aware of your body language

Strange as it sounds, your body language in a telephone conversation will affect the tone of your voice and will influence the interviewer's perception of you. Make sure that you are sitting upright in a comfortable chair and keep your chin up when you are speaking. If your back is straight it will allow you to breathe slowly and deeply, your raised chin will prevent you from mumbling and will increase your confidence. Try speaking with a friend when you are slouching and then change your posture as suggested above. I will bet that your friend comments on how your voice sounds clearer and more confident.

Avoid walking around

This is especially important if you do decide to receive the call on your mobile. Not only can you lose reception, but the fact that you are 'on the move' can make you appear distracted and uneasy.

Charlie's chapter tips:

- Find a comfortable place to receive the call.

- Turn off your mobile, TV and stereo.

- Give the company a landline number.

- Prepare as you would for a face-to-face interview.

- Be by your phone at the agreed time.

- Smile.

- Use professional, positive language.

- Sit upright in your chair.

- Carpe Diem': let's seize the day and so move into role play!

Chapter 8

Presentations, assessment centres & role plays

"Whatever you do, do it to the purpose; do it thoroughly, not superficially. Go to the bottom of things. Anything half done, or half known, is in my mind, neither done nor known at all."

Lord Chesterfield

If you are successful in your first interview many organisations will ask you back to present a topic to key members of staff; sometimes these will be members of the team you could be working with. Certain organisations combine this with role plays and further interviews in what is called an Assessment Centre. These assessment days will often involve other candidates in group exercises, and therefore you need to plan how you are going to communicate with people who may be competing with you for the same job. The following chapter will help you prepare for what can be quite an exhausting experience.

Expect the unexpected

If you have been put forward by an agency ask them to provide you with details of what to expect on the day. A good agency will want to provide you with as much support as possible and therefore should pass on comprehensive information on timings, topics and how you will be assessed. If you have applied direct to a company they should provide you with similar information. Don't be surprised if some of the exercises you are expected to perform are not on this list. Sometimes organisations will want to see how you cope with the unexpected. If this happens, take a deep breath, keep your composure and remember that often the company is more interested in how you react rather than the content of your response.

Read the question twice and then read it again

If you are required to make a presentation it is imperative that you understand what is being asked of you. Although the organisation is going to focus on how you deliver and communicate the message, they will also assess how successfully you have understood and answered the question. I have seen many candidates deliver wonderful presentations that have unfortunately been very loosely based on the original topic.

Brainstorm

Once you understand the key questions the presentation title requires you to answer, it is a good idea to take a large piece of paper and start to write down all your thoughts and views concerning the title. Allowing yourself to empty your mind of all the thoughts associated with the title helps you build the content. If you attempt to plan the structure before you have gone through this process you will be in danger of missing important information and getting too bogged down by detail too early.

Chapter 8

Read the question again

Déjà vu? I know that I have given this tip previously but now you are ready to build the content it is vital that you revisit the title so that you are certain that you are on target.

Clear as a bell

Once you have got all your ideas down on the page you are then in a position to organise them into appropriate sections. During this stage it is important to be clear about how you are going to answer the question and how you are going to best communicate this to the audience. Avoid unnecessary complexity. Keep your statements clear and unambiguous.

Beware the shibboleth

A shibboleth is another expression for jargon and should be avoided because you could be in danger of alienating your audience. Always keep in the forefront of your mind the fact that you want to connect with the people in the room. Therefore use language that your audience is going to appreciate and understand. There is a preconception about having to use 'business speech' during interviews and if you regularly watch *The Apprentice* you know what I mean. You will often find that the people using 'business speech' are actually hiding the fact that they don't know what they are talking about! You are looking to build rapport with the client and therefore unnecessary jargon should be avoided at all costs.

PC or flipchart

To avoid the David Brent approach, I strongly advise that you create a PowerPoint presentation. If you are not competent using this software than find a friend who is, and sit with them when they put the presentation together. The majority of organisations will expect you to deliver it in this format and it also allows you to be much more creative in how you convey the information to the audience.

Images

Using images instead of words can be a very powerful way to communicate your message. If you feel that this strategy isn't appropriate ensure that you don't overload the slides with too much detail. Three to four main points per slide is more than adequate.

Gunshots and whip cracks

If you have worked with PowerPoint then you will know that you can create all kinds of weird and wonderful sound effects as words appear on the screen. Although this is extremely tempting as a way of 'livening up' your presentation, gun shots and sirens are probably not the most suitable for a formal presentation. Consider the role and the company as you create the presentation and ask yourself (or someone else if your view is rather warped!) whether you really feel it is appropriate for their environment. If you feel that the audience would appreciate a more lively presentation then go for it!

Fades and shuttering

As with sound, you can also create effects as you move from one page of the presentation to the other. Choose something very simple that will not detract from the subject matter. In the majority of presentations, unless you are interviewing for a creative position, it is the content that is the most important rather than your PowerPoint expertise.

Uniformity

A presentation is like a CV in many ways. It needs to be something that is easy to follow and attractive to the eye. To help with this it is advisable to use the same font throughout as well as the same methods for bringing information onto the screen. I don't want to inhibit your creativity (there is much more freedom for positions that are more creative and design-focused) but merely to point out that on the whole a presentation with a degree of uniformity is going to be easier to follow and will look much more professional.

Practise makes perfect

As with all things the more you practise the better you will become. An interview can be a stressful experience and therefore we need to do everything we can to reduce this potential anxiety. I strongly recommend that you practise reading your presentation out loud, firstly to yourself and then to an audience. There is nothing like hearing the words spoken out loud to highlight the strengths and the areas for further improvement. Swallow your pride and ask for feedback. The more times you practise going through the presentation the more confidence you will have when you do it for real.

Time and tide wait for no man

As well as a defined subject the organisation will also set a time limit for your presentation. This is not a 'suggestion', this is the maximum time they will sit there listening to you, so go beyond this at your peril! This is why practise is so important. If your presentation is longer than the allotted time it shows poor awareness and a lack of preparation and is very likely to harm your application.

Technical failure

Technology is a wonderful thing but it isn't foolproof. Without attracting failure it is wise to have a contingency plan if the worst happens. It is an extremely good idea to have printouts of your presentation ready in case the PC crashes or the presentation doesn't load properly. I suggest that you only hand these out if this occurs since you don't want your audience to be looking at bits of paper when they should be looking at you.

Technical support

Even if you are a technical wizard it is wise to check with the company whether there will be someone there to help you set up the presentation. This is another tip aimed at reducing the number of 'unknowns' thus reducing any feelings of anxiety. If you have practised your presentation well, you are armed with printouts and you know exactly what to expect on the day then you are on the right path for success.

Don't drone or be a monotone

However fascinating your content might be most people will lose interest if you deliver your presentation in one tone of voice. Have a think about people who excite you and capture your imagination. What makes them inspirational? Is it what they say or how they say it? What is most important? I would say that how you deliver a message is often more important than the message itself. I am not suggesting that you should alter your personality but that you should allow your personality to express itself. If you understand your content well you will know which parts need to be accentuated and made more colourful.

The 'ayes' have it…

Whereas an interview may involve one representative from a company, a presentation will often involve a panel of people all eager to listen to your words of wisdom. Remember that no-one likes feeling left out and so make a point of engaging the whole audience. As you are delivering your content ensure that you make eye contact with all of the members of the panel – this makes each person feel that you are directing your message to them. Try not to dwell on one person for too long, instead move naturally from one person to the next.

If you are wise you will summarise

We have already stated that the point of a presentation is to answer a question or prove a statement to be true or untrue. Therefore you should end your presentation with a summary that brings your key points together and concludes the main point you are making. This doesn't need to be a lengthy close but a paragraph that highlights your most important points.

Prepare to be examined

It is highly likely that the company will want to ask you questions about your presentation and the points that you have made. These tend to come at the end but sometimes one or more of the panel will want to ask questions during the presentation itself. Have a think about what they are likely to ask you and plan how you are going to answer. Remember that not all questions have a yes or a no answer, so consider your responses carefully.

Notes are merely a guide

We have already talked about the importance of maintaining eye contact and therefore continually referring to notes can act as a distraction to your audience. Your notes are there as a guide so that you keep on track. If you have practised your presentation well (as I know you will have!) you will be able to talk confidently without needing notes. This also helps with voice projection since your head and chin will be raised when you are speaking.

To thine own self be true

Borrowing the words of William Shakespeare, in all the decisions and actions in your life it is important to be true to yourself. This can seem challenging in assessment centres and especially during group exercises when assessors will be analysing how the members of a team interact. Ask yourself if you would prefer to be judged as yourself or as the person you think they want you to be? By being yourself, you are more likely to appear natural and confident and furthermore you are much more likely to secure the job that is right for you.

Remember The Apprentice

If you have watched *The Apprentice* I am sure that you have cringed at the way that some of the contestants behave during group exercises. Like in life, the business world is competitive but that doesn't mean that you have to forego all decency just to succeed. The manner in which you interact with people in a highly competitive environment will be being monitored by the assessors. Reaching the top is virtually impossible without the support and guidance of others so make sure that you treat others as you would like to be treated.

Do unto others…

Without wanting to appear moralistic, although I am conscious that this chapter is heading that way, it is important to respect the views and opinions of the other team members during a group exercise even if you fundamentally disagree with them. The whole point of group exercises is for the client to observe how you react in a team of people with different personalities and opinions. They will be noting the following: Who are the natural leaders? Who are team players? How do people react when their views are not acted upon? Who are the dominating personalities? How do people react when this type of individual takes control? Always keep your cool and your emotions under control.

No-one likes a sulker

You are quite within your rights to make your point firmly and confidently within a group but if your opinion isn't acted on don't start sulking! Move on and make sure that you continue to make a positive impact on the task in hand even if the task is not successful. The assessors will be looking at how people react and cope with conflict and disappointment.

Avoid blinkers

During a group exercise it can be very easy to become too focussed on the task and the objectives. Keep you wits about you and give yourself time to observe and listen to what is happening around you. Don't fall into the trap, as others around you may do, of feeling that you have to dive into the task immediately. Often it is wise to observe what is going on, formulate a suitable plan and then confidently suggest this to the team.

Show enthusiasm

As the great Ralph Waldo Emerson wrote "Nothing great was ever achieved without enthusiasm." It is infectious and makes good things happen. Create a positive energy in the group and show a willingness to get things done.

What is role play?

Companies will sometimes create a work scenario that you will encounter in the job. This could involve a simulated sales pitch where you play the part of the salesperson and the client acts out the role of the customer. The purpose of role play is to see how you react and perform in a situation that is close to real life. Although it is an unnatural environment the secret is to swallow any feelings of embarrassment and attack the exercise with total commitment. Imagine that this is a real life situation and act accordingly.

Understand your role

I am not suggesting that you need to research the motivations of your character or to arrive to the interview with props; a method acting approach really is unnecessary. But you will need to be clear about what the situation is and your relationship with the role played by the client. Being able to put the role play into context helps you to act in a believable manner.

Remember the competencies

Start thinking about what competencies the company will be assessing you on. If you are interviewing for a customer service role it is likely that during your role play they will be listening out for your ability to show empathy, the ability to build rapport, to problem-solve and to demonstrate good listening skills.

Don't promise the world

Some candidates make the mistake of making unrealistic commitments during a role play exercise. This can be an easy error to make since it is not a real-life scenario. Always keep in mind what you would be happy to commit to if you were performing the role for real, and be consistent.

Big Brother is watching you

With an assessment centre you are always being assessed. This doesn't end with the conclusion of the individual exercises and it is wise to remember this during the periods in between the tasks. Be mindful of the language you use and how you communicate with the other candidates.

Temper your temper

Throughout the whole interview process remember to always keep your temper. You might spend a whole day at an assessment centre and the pressure of problem-solving tasks, group exercises and role plays can take its toll. Whatever happens, even if you cannot agree with any of the people in your team, smile and maintain your sense of humour.

Charlie's chapter tips:

- When you plan your presentation read the question and then read it again.

- Create a clear PowerPoint presentation and avoid strange sound effects.

- Practise delivering your presentation to an audience.

- Keep to the time limit.

- Be yourself and respect the opinions of others.

- Keep your temper and your sense of humour.

- Remember that you are always being assessed.

- Show your enthusiasm.

- You've learnt at quite a pace and now it's time for the face-to-face!

Chapter 9

Face-to-face interviews

> "Only I can change my life. No one can do it for me."
>
> **Carol Burnett**

The time for preparation is over and it is the day of the interview. It is now time to put the meat on the bones. This section provides useful tips on how to behave during the interview itself.

Respect the gate-keeper

Remember that the interview starts as soon as you walk through the company's doors and not just when you are in the interview room. Greet the staff at reception with a smile and confidently and politely introduce yourself.

Remember Trigger Happy TV

To avoid any highly embarrassing 'Crazy Frog' ringtone incidences please remember to turn off your mobile phone. There are few things more annoying than a mobile going off at an inappropriate time and it will really shatter your composure.

Body language

An interviewer will not only be assessing you on what you say but also on what you don't say; 55% of first impressions are based on visual impact (appearance, facial expressions and body language) and 38% on the tone of your voice. This only leaves 7% to be based on what you actually say.

Smile

A warm smile never hurt anyone. Smiling helps to build rapport with the interviewer and can also help to ease nerves. As with most things, avoid over-doing it – smiling constantly like a Cheshire cat could result in a white coat escort out of the building!

Facial expressions

Expressions help to show the interviewer that you are listening and they assist with building rapport (we will cover this in more detail later in this chapter). Note comments in the previous tip: although you should be aware of your expressions, they should also be natural, otherwise you may see some strange expressions on the interviewer's face.

Firm but fair

A firm handshake with good eye contact generates a feeling of confidence and reliability. The correct method is to allow your hand to grasp the fleshy part of the other person's hand (not the fingers), squeeze firmly and then shake up and down two or three times. 'Wet fish' or 'bone-crusher' handshakes are to be avoided.

Pregnant pauses…

A common mistake that interviewees make is feeling that they have to fill in pauses in conversation. Silence can be golden, even in an interview. The secret of using pauses effectively is to maintain eye contact with the interviewer. When you feel that you have given enough detail in an answer, pause and hand control back to the interviewer. If they feel that they need further information from you they will either remain silent or will ask you to elaborate on your answer. By being aware of the interviewer's reaction to your pauses you gain valuable information on whether your answers are too short or too lengthy.

And the punch line is…

Never ever complete an interviewer's sentence, even if you have to bite your lip in order to stay silent! They might be speaking at a snail's pace, but always remember that they are the ones ultimately responsible for hiring you or not.

Honesty is the best policy

Someone wise once said "If you tell the truth, you never have to remember anything". If you think about it, it makes perfect sense! An interviewer will be studying your mannerisms, your tone of voice as well as the content of what you are saying and if you start to massage the truth there is a good chance that they will spot it. An interview is all about building rapport and trust. If you are caught lying during an interview, the interviewer will assume that you would probably lie in the job. Be brave and stick to the facts.

Acting the chameleon

A recent survey suggested that a third of employees have admitted to acting in an interview, purely to try and fit into their perception of the company culture. Suggesting that you should be 'yourself' might seem an implausible request since an interview can be a very unnatural environment, but hiding your true self can cause problems further down the line. It may be that your personality doesn't mesh well with the team or the company culture and that doesn't help you or the company. It can also be very stressful for you if you have to 'act' whilst at work. Do not fear, as you are not alone. The same survey revealed that many employees discovered a different side to their managers' personalities from the ones they experienced at interview! It is important to note that 'acting' is very different from 'adapting' your personality, and we will cover this later in this chapter.

Assumption is the feast of fools

There is a slightly more Anglo-Saxon version of this phrase that I know would have prevented this book being published! However, the message is not to assume anything because you will often be wrong. Just because your interviewer may be nodding and smiling doesn't automatically mean that he/she is agreeing with you. Remain on your toes and don't get too cocky.

!!~**!!*!

To avoid your mouth being washed out with soap and water, keep your language clean! This might sound obvious, but some interviews can become quite 'informal' and even the interviewer may swear. Be very careful not to feel you have to mirror their language, because you may overdo it. It may be that you have built such a great rapport with the interviewer that you are both able to be more relaxed but my rule of thumb would be avoid swear words full stop (unless you are being interviewed by Gordon Ramsey!).

Chapter 9

Humour or deadpan?

Some interviews can be rather clinical, and stuffy. A touch of humour can lighten the moment, build rapport and be an opportunity for your personality to shine through. It can also be dangerous. Humour in the wrong context can be a disaster. The important aspects to take into consideration are: Are you naturally a humorous person? If so, then this will come out without needing to be conscious about it and you can just add a sprinkling of humour at the right times and in the right places. If you are not a naturally funny person, the best advice is don't try to be. Just build rapport in other ways, such as through the sincerity of your responses and in your ability to understand the client's questions. It is also important when using humour to assess the personality of your interviewer and the requirements of the job.

Shoes off by the door

One way to make sure that you behave in an appropriate manner during an interview is to imagine that you are a guest in a stranger's home. Okay, taking your shoes off and leaving them outside the door is taking it a step too far (!) but arriving with this mindset will help to put politeness at the forefront of your mind.

Step into their shoes

Another technique is to imagine that you are the interviewer. If you were in their shoes, ask yourself what behaviour from you would seem appropriate or inappropriate in the context of the situation. As well as the physical behaviour, consider what language would inspire confidence and trust.

Think before you speak

In the heat and pressure of the interview thought processes can become muddled. The last thing you want to do is to make some statement that sends you down a blind alley or that makes you divulge information you would rather have kept to yourself. A very simple technique is to pause, take a breath and then gather your thoughts before answering particularly challenging questions. This technique can also be used to avoid sounding as if your answers are all pre-planned.

What is rapport?

Rapport building is all about creating a perception of mutual respect and understanding between two or more people. This sense of understanding can be created via what we say but also by our body language. In the majority of cases we develop rapport without thinking; for example if a friend turns their head to speak with you, you will probably turn your head to face them as well without even thinking. The challenge is that in stressful situations, such as interviews, we can become so concerned with what we are going to say that we can miss the opportunity to build rapport through our body language.

Rapport building

At the heart of every interview is the question Can I work with this person? If we think about it most of our most successful relationships, whether that be with friends or family, are based on whether you like spending time in that person's company. This is the case with most interviews and by being aware of this you should focus on the value of building a good level of rapport (although with some careers the need for certain skill sets outweighs the desire for a certain personality type).

Family focused or adrenalin junky

You can tell a lot about an interviewer by what is on their desk and this is when being 'aware' during an interview can be used to your advantage. As you walk into the person's office glance at what is on their desk and walls. Do they have photos of family, sporting images or personal awards? Is their desk tidy or cluttered? All of this information can help to create an impression of what their personality might be like and what subjects you might be able to slip into the conversation in order to build rapport.

Mirror, mirror on the wall

Another clever way to build rapport with your interviewer is to listen to the language they use. It is possible to use similar language in a subtle way in order to make them feel that you are on their wavelength. Some people have a preference to the way that they describe things. For example, they might say that they feel something…, whilst others may say that they think something…. By being able to mirror some of the terms that they use you can build rapport more quickly. Don't overdo this though as it will start to appear unnatural.

Hands where they can be seen

Whether you are a very expressive person or not, it is best to keep your hands either on the table, on the arms of the chair or resting on your lap. What to do with your hands is a dilemma that many people have in all kinds of social situations. The secret is to be aware of what comes naturally to you and don't try to wave them about like a conductor if this is not your normal manner! It is quite acceptable to have your hands folded or resting on your lap or on the table. Having your hands in view of your interviewer is another way of appearing to be more open.

How to sit in a chair

I promise you that I am not trying to insult your intelligence; some people are not aware of how important this can be. The way that you sit is another way an interviewer can get a sense of your personality. It is very easy to portray the wrong image, often through nerves. If you lean too far back you can appear arrogant and if you lean too far forward you can appear confrontational. Naturally, it is vital to be comfortable and then to sit as upright in the chair as you can. You can move position as the interview progresses and as you start to build rapport with the interviewer. Try to avoid striking the pose with hands behind your head combined with feet on the desk!

Look into my eyes

Eye contact is crucial when you are looking to build rapport with your interviewer. When used well, good eye contact can create feelings of confidence, trust and understanding. Don't overdo it though. An unblinking 'Medusa stare' is not very friendly. Your eyes will naturally move around when you are recalling information but if you look away or down at the floor for long periods of time during an interview it can raise suspicions in the interviewer's mind about your honesty and or your confidence.

Look interested

Many interviewees forget this very simple fact, often because of nervousness. Remember that the interviewer is scrutinising every little facial gesture and the subtle changes in the tone of your voice. Demonstrate your interest, your enthusiasm and your energy with positive body language and with passion in your voice. I realise that I have highlighted that you need to be 'in control' of what you say but in the same breath don't be afraid to display emotion.

Note taking

I must admit that I am not a great fan of candidates taking notes during an interview. For me it is similar to referring to your CV during an interview, it breaks eye contact and is a distraction. If you really feel you have to take notes, at least ask the interviewer beforehand to see whether they are happy for you to do so.

Facing an interview panel

Many organisations will adopt an interview panel approach to interviewing. In this instance you could be asked to field questions from two or more interviewers and clearly this creates different challenges from a one-on-one interview. The following tips will guide you safely through this potential minefield.

Include all parties

In the heat of the interview it is very easy to forget that there are other people present in the room and you can end up directing all your answers to one person. Even if one individual appears to be leading the interview and asking the majority of questions, it is vital to include all parties in your answers. Begin by initially forming eye contact with the person who asked the question and then move your eyes so that you create rapport with the other individuals in turn.

Keep your body central to the interviewers

Ensure that your posture in the chair allows you to engage with and to be engaged by all parties in the room. Avoid turning your body or head away in a way that closes you off from the other interviewers.

Why is this so important?

In very simple terms nobody likes to feel left out or ignored! If we look at it more closely, it could be that your potential boss is the one who is observing rather than asking the questions. If they feel that you have excluded them from the interview it raises serious questions about your awareness of others.

Nerves are fine

Many international sportspeople will tell you that they feel 'butterflies in the stomach' or even 'fear' before a major event. Being nervous before an interview is natural and is often a good thing because it means that the result of it matters to you. I assure you that in some cases even the interviewer is nervous! The best antidote to fear is preparation. If you have prepared well then you have little to fear.

Deep breaths

Another tip is to slow your breathing down when you are waiting in reception; by breathing deeply you will slow your racing heart and feel more in control. I remember one of my first ever interviews for a job with a recruitment company in London. I was being interviewed by the Manager of the Permanent Division and we were in the 'ice-breaking' stage when he asked if I wanted a coffee. I had to refuse it since my shakes were so bad I would have hurled the contents around the room!

Thank you notes

If you were forced to write to Aunts and Uncles thanking them for their Christmas presents this will probably be second nature to you. It can be a nice gesture to email or write a letter to the person who interviewed you thanking them for their time and restating your interest in the opportunity. If you have been put forward by an agency it is polite to let the Consultant know that you intend to do this.

Top ten tips for disastrous interviews (please don't add to this list!):

1. Smelling of alcohol!

2. Turning up to the wrong office.

3. Arriving late.

4. Forgetting the name of the person or people interviewing you.

5. An inability to describe what the company does.

6. Not knowing the key responsibilities of the role.

7. Not being able to talk through your CV.

8. Being unable to answer the question "Why

do you want this job?"

9. Arriving on the wrong day.

10. Being rude or confrontational during the interview.

Top ten tips for successful interviews:

1. Researching the company's financial figures. Often these will be on the company website. If not, call the company direct to obtain them.

2. Getting the inside track from someone performing the same role in the company or someone in a similar role with a competitor.

3. Calmly arriving for the interview with plenty of time, smartly dressed and with a polite greeting for reception.

4. Drawing up a proposal that outlines what you will be able to bring to the business in terms of creative ideas and revenue.

5. Listen. This will enable you to pick up on valuable signs from the interviewer that could make the difference between success and failure.

6. The ability to read the body language of the interviewer so that you know when you are talking too much or not enough.

7. Showing enthusiasm.

8. Honesty. I cannot stress enough how important this is. If the interviewer detects the slightest signal that you are not being honest, you could be waving

goodbye to that once in a lifetime opportunity.

9. Self-awareness and the confidence to admit to weaknesses and mistakes.

10. A strong belief in your own ability.

Charlie's chapter tips:

1. Your interview starts as soon as you walk through the office doors.

2. Make sure all electrical items are switched off before a telephone interview!

3. Smile.

4. Mind your language.

5. Think before you speak.

6. Listen.

7. Answer with enthusiasm.

8. Maintain good eye contact.

9. As long as you haven't stepped out of line you are now prepared for offer time!

Why are Manhole Covers Round?

Chapter 10

Decision time

> "Think like a wise man but communicate in the language of the people."
>
> **William Butler Yeats**

Congratulations! Start Monday! This is what we would all like to hear at the end of an interview but sometimes it is possible to talk ourselves out of a possible job offer because we feel uncomfortable about handling 'the close'. This section covers the areas of salary negotiations and how to make your interest clear without appearing too pushy.

Greed is good... or is it?

Even Gordon Gekko got this wrong in the end! It is natural to want to earn more than your previous job but don't price yourself out of the market. Remember, if you are asking for a substantial increase you must be confident in your ability to warrant this rise and more importantly you must be able to present a solid argument to the client as to why they should pay this figure.

So, do you like me or not?

It is perfectly natural to want feedback from the interviewer immediately after an interview, and there are different schools of thought on this subject. The recommended option is to test the waters by asking the interviewer what the next stage would be whilst also stating your interest in the position. This allows the interviewer to decide whether to offer their feedback then and there, or to just provide you with an outline of what might happen if successful. Bear in mind that the company might have seen five or six candidates in one day and therefore many clients will want to consider their thoughts before coming back with a definitive answer.

Handling the salary issue

For some people talking about money can be uncomfortable. If you are going through an agency your consultant will often advise you, however it will frequently come up during the interview. The best advice is to answer confidently and back up your comments with examples of where you can add value to your potential employer. If challenged, these examples should enable the interviewer to gain a clear picture of what you did in your previous role as well as the experience and skills that you can bring to them that will warrant the level of salary you desire.

Know your figures

If you know what salary and package are being offered for the position and you are asked directly what salary or package you are seeking then it is imperative that you are clear about what that figure is. If you don't know your own worth you can't expect your interviewer to do that for you. If the package is not made clear to you then it is acceptable for you to ask more detail from the client before making a commitment about your own salary expectations.

Chapter 10

Asking questions

In the majority of interviews, there will be time at the end for you to ask the interviewer questions. I strongly advise you to plan these before the interview otherwise you could be in danger of talking yourself out of the position. Ask yourself what you feel you need to know about the role and the company that isn't clear from the job specification or website. Example questions might be What are the long term career opportunities within this area of the business? or I see that the company has recently made an acquisition. What effect might this have on this particular team? If you feel that these questions have already been answered during the course of the interview, then let the interviewer know so that they are aware that you had taken the time to plan questions.

A time for reflection

After your interview (and when your heartbeat has returned to its normal rhythm!) it is a worthwhile exercise to review how you think you performed. This is useful for many different reasons: you can learn from any mistakes, which will stand you in good stead for future interviews, and it helps you to prepare for a possible second interview with the same organisation, especially if you recognise certain areas that you feel they may probe further. The best way to do this is to write down your thoughts and observations. To make it clear you could divide a page into three columns of what you did well, what you could improve and areas you feel you may need to research further for subsequent interviews.

Feedback session

If your interview was organised through a recruitment consultant it is usual that you will be required to call the Consultant with your feedback immediately after the interview. Even if you feel the interview went poorly, or if you feel that it is the wrong job for you, make sure that you still give them a call.

Planning for second interviews

If you have gone through an agency the recruitment consultant should be able to provide you with an outline of the second interview process. It is likely that new faces will be involved and in some instances it might be a different panel altogether. The key thing to remember is to find out as much information about the second interview as you can and then carry out the necessary research.

Further probing

With many companies the first interview is focused on understanding whether you have the ability to perform the role and whether you will be a good fit within their team and organisation. The second interview is when things get a bit more serious. It is likely to involve more probing questions covering your experience as well as scenario-based questions to see how you approach problems. The secret is to think hard about what they are likely to ask in relation to the role's responsibilities and then plan how you are going to use examples to demonstrate your suitability.

Answer out loud

A really good tip is to say your answers out loud to a friend. Ask them whether you sound convincing. Do you sound confident and convincing to yourself? Are you comfortable with the language and detail of your answers?

Projection is perception

What we say, the manner in which we say it and the posture we adopt has a direct impact on how we are perceived by others. If you don't believe me, listen closely to sportspeople when they are being interviewed after a successful performance. Listen to the language that they use. If they have played well they are certainly not shy in telling us about it! Successful people use powerful words that inspire and empower so think about how you want to be seen and act as if you are that person already.

Company research

As well as asking more searching questions about your own experience, the interviewer is also likely to ask you more challenging questions about their own organisation. I know that I already sound like a broken record but I cannot over emphasise the need for thorough company research. Investigate the company's performance, look at the annual report, understand their business strategy and know how the company is perceived by its customers and competitors.

A penny for your thoughts

You could well be asked your opinion of the organisation's services or even whether you could recommend areas for improvement. This question gives you quite a lot of rope and if you are not careful you could hang yourself with it! Ensure that your comments are positive and if you feel you need to highlight areas of weakness then make your comments constructive. The only way to be able to answer these questions confidently and in a convincing fashion is by carrying out the proper research.

Building relationships

It is important to remember that even if your first interview went without incident and you managed to develop a good rapport with one or more of the interviewers, beware of complacency. Start the second interview with the same freshness and enthusiasm as the first but arm yourself with more detail on the company.

Dealing with offers

It is unusual for a company to make an offer on the spot but if they do you needn't feel under pressure to make a decision then and there. The majority of organisations will appreciate that accepting a new job is a big decision and one that can impact on other people's lives as well as your own. You may need to discuss the offer with your parents or your partner. My advice is to state your interest in the offer and then say that you will need time to consider it properly. It is polite to give the company a time when you will come back with an answer; 24 hours to a week is acceptable, any longer and companies will begin to lose patience.

Turning offers down

After attending one or more interviews you may actually feel that the role just isn't for you. This could be for a number of different reasons. The important thing is to analyse your doubts about the opportunity so that you are happy with your decision. It is then important to make the company and recruitment agency aware of your decision as soon as you have made it. Remember that your decision impacts on the company and therefore they will appreciate knowing your decision quickly as well as the reasons behind it.

Handling the notice period

Some companies might wish you to join before you finish your notice period with your current employer. Again, don't feel pressurised to take any action that you are not comfortable with. The best approach is to state the length of your notice period and then to add that you will discuss a reduced period of time with your current employer but that the final decision is theirs. Remember that this course of action actually displays a level of maturity and an appreciation of your responsibilities that can only be seen as being positive. How you act towards your current employer is how you are likely to behave towards your future employer and is an indication of your level of integrity.

Charlie's chapter tips:

- Justify your worth with evidence of your achievements.

- Don't push too hard for the interviewer's opinion of you.

- Ask considered questions that you have planned before the day.

- Review your performance and learn from any mistakes.

- Prepare even more thoroughly for second interviews.

- If you are going through a recruitment agency discuss your feedback with the Consultant.

- Take your time to consider offers carefully and let the company know when you will make a decision.

- Congratulations and adieu! An exciting future awaits you!

Useful websites:

www.prospects.ac.uk – is the UK's official graduate careers website and the leading provider of information, advice and opportunities to students and graduates.

www.jobsite.co.uk – is a leading UK online recruitment site covering opportunities across a variety of different sectors.

www.jobserve.com – were the world's first internet recruitment service, now operating across 17 different industry sectors.

www.monster.co.uk – is a leading provider of online careers and recruitment resources.

www.cipd.co.uk – is the website for the Chartered Institute of Personnel and Development and a useful resource for information on training and changes in legislation.

www.recruiter.co.uk – is the website for the Recruiter magazine, the principle magazine for UK recruitment profession, providing you with free access to their content.

www.bemyinterviewer.co.uk – This is really excellent! It is part of the Jobsite UK Group, and enables you to watch online video clips of leading people in the commercial world presenting their best interview tips.

www.learndirect-advice.co.uk – is a site offering practical advice to help you make the right career choices.

www.reed.co.uk – was the first recruitment site offered

by a recruitment agency in the UK and has now developed into one the UK's leading job sites.

www.connexions.gov.uk – provides information and help for young people on topics that include careers, learning, work and money.

www.careerbuilder.co.uk – is a leading jobs, careers and employment website.

www.interviewgold.com – is an interactive online system that teaches people how to prepare for various styles and stages of interview.

www.targetjobs.co.uk – a graduate opportunities website that also provides careers intelligence.

www.jobcentreplus.gov.uk – is a government agency tasked with helping people from welfare into work, as well as helping employers fill their vacancies.

The Author

Charlie Mulraine is a *Career Transition Mentor* helping elite athletes and individuals in commerce continue their success in new directions.

A former professional rugby player and cricketer, for the past 10 years Charlie has supported the Professional Cricketers' Association's work placement scheme creating off season career opportunities for many current and former players within industry. He has also worked in premiership rugby and professional football where he has presented to the Manchester United squad on the challenges of life after professional sport.

His *Dream Believe and Achieve* and *Live your Mission* workshops use principles from elite sport to help people find their true purpose and potential.

Charlie lives near Stratford-upon-Avon with his wife and family. Still a keen sportsman, Charlie spends much of his free time on his bike riding charity sportives.

More information can be found at:

www.mulrainesport.com
Career Transition Strategy for Sportspeople

www.thepca.co.uk
The Professional Cricketers' Association

For FREE tips and advice go to Charlie's Blog
http://myminutementor.wordpress.com

Lightning Source UK Ltd.
Milton Keynes UK
UKOW04f0512081014

239750UK00001BA/5/P